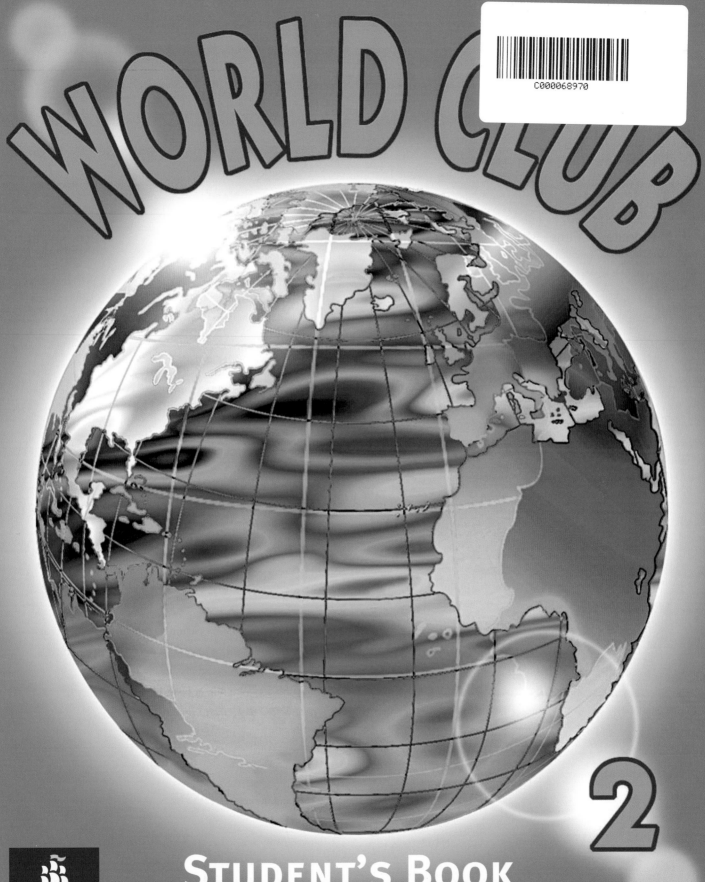

WORLD CLUB

2

STUDENT'S BOOK

Michael Harris   David Mower

Longman

CONTENTS MAP

Learning to learn

A Using World Club

a

Match the modules with the photos.

1 Animals   5 Spies

2 Homes   6 Food

3 Stories   7 Tomorrow's World

4 Stars   8 Machines

b

True or false? Look through *World Club 2*.

1 The lead-in page for *Animals* has got a photo of a lion.

2 The *Language Focus* in Lesson 4 is about prepositions.

3 The title of Lesson 13 is *Mission Anaconda*.

4 The *Writing* in Module 5 *Fluency* is a story.

5 The *Consolidation* for Module 8 is on page 85.

6 The *Module Check* for Module 1 has got five questions.

c

In pairs, ask and answer questions about the book.

Example: A: What page is Lesson 22 on?

        B: It's on page 78. Who is the film star in Lesson 10?

        A: It's Kate Winslet.

B Your Learning

a

Look at the questionnaire. Listen to José and write down his answers.

1 Why do you think it is important to learn English?

  a for travel

  b for work

  c for study

2 Evaluate these classroom activities:

- speaking in English with my partner
- listening to cassettes
- watching videos
- reading stories
- listening to songs
- doing grammar exercises
- doing tests
- playing games

    a very interesting

    b OK

    c not very interesting

3 Which of these things do you do in English?

  a listen to pop songs

  b watch films in English

  c read books in English

4 Give yourself a mark out of ten for:

  a speaking   **e** writing

  b listening   **f** vocabulary

  c grammar   **g** pronunciation

  d reading

b

Answer the questionnaire yourself.

c

In pairs, interview your partner. Write down his/her results.

d

Look at the two ways of organising vocabulary: alphabetically and by topic.

Organise the words below in the same way. There are five topics.

- school
- food
- animals
- homes
- machines

school

sandwich / bedroom / blackboard / teacher / kitchen / classroom / cat / bathroom / car / hamburger / lion / television / zebra / apple / computer

C School Reports

a

Read the reports. Which of the students:

1 is good at speaking and listening?

2 is good at writing and grammar?

3 has got a good vocabulary book?

4 has problems with grammar?

5 sometimes does not do homework?

6 does not speak English in class?

Example: 1 Carlos

b 🔑 KEYWORDS

Which of these words are similar in your language?

> excellent problems disorganised untidy
> hard organised tidy try

Read the reports again and use the mini-dictionary to find the meaning of other words.

c

Make a list of new words from this module. In pairs, test your partner.

Example: A: What does 'star' mean in our language?

   B: It is ...

   A: How do you spell it?

   B: s – t – a – r

d

Write a short report about your English. Give it to your teacher.

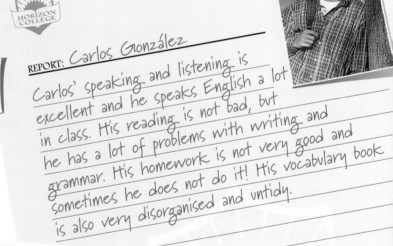

REPORT: Carlos González

Carlos' speaking and listening is excellent and he speaks English a lot in class. His reading is not bad, but he has a lot of problems with writing and grammar. His homework is not very good and sometimes he does not do it! His vocabulary book is also very disorganised and untidy.

REPORT: Magda Grotowski

Magda works hard in class and her homework is always very good. Her grammar and writing tests are excellent. Her vocabulary book is also very organised and tidy. Magda's problem is her speaking and listening. She does not try to speak English in class.

ANIMALS
Lead-in

MODULE OBJECTIVES

IN THIS MODULE YOU WILL ...

Read	about nasty pets and Australian animals.
Listen	to an animal quiz and a story.
Talk	about animals and pets.
Practise	the present simple tense.
Write	a description of a real or invented animal.

Busy bees at work.

The south American fruit bat having lunch.

a   KEYWORDS

Classify the animals in the photos and in the box. Use the mini-dictionary to help you.

> elephant eagle snake dolphin ant
> chameleon cockroach ostrich lizard

The smile of the Nile crocodile.

b

In pairs, add other animals to the lists. Tell the class.

Example: A chimpanzee is a mammal.

Example:

Mammals	Reptiles	Birds	Insects
elephant			

Emperor Penguins going for a walk.

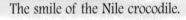

1 Nasty Pets

A KEYWORDS

What is your opinion of the animals in the photos? Tell the class.

Example: I think ants are nice.

> lovely nice OK horrible
> not very nice
> absolutely revolting

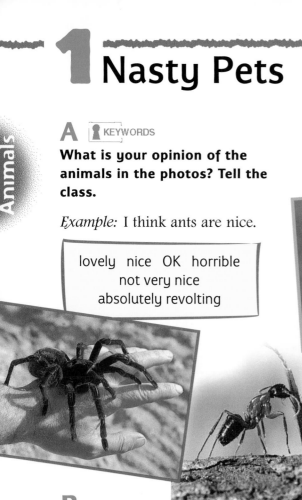

B

Are these facts about redback spiders (RS) or cockroaches (C)? Use the mini-dictionary.

Example: 1 RS

1 They live under toilet seats.
2 They live inside TVs.
3 They love bathrooms.
4 They eat everything.
5 They bite and kill people.
6 They don't like lights.
7 They sleep in the day and come out at night.
8 They can run fast.

C

Read the texts and check your answers in exercise B.

Redback spiders are from Australia. They love bathrooms and live under toilet seats. Redbacks hate people sitting on them. They bite and they have an easy target! Every year they kill people in Australia. Redbacks do not make good pets!

Cockroaches eat everything. They often live inside TVs where they eat cables and listen to Cartoon Network. Cockroaches sleep in the day and come out at night. When you want to see one, put food on the kitchen floor. At night, go into the kitchen and switch on the light. Cockroaches don't like lights and try to escape. Move fast if you want to catch one in your hand.

Language Focus: Present Simple

D

Copy and complete the tables.

AFFIRMATIVE		
I / you / we / they	¹ ...	under toilet seats.
He / she / it	lives	in Australia.

NEGATIVE		
I / you / we / they	² ... (don't)	under toilet seats.
He / she / it	**does not** live (doesn't)	in Australia.

See Grammar Reference 1 on page 16.

E

Complete the sentences.

Example: 1 My sister does not like rats.

1 My sister (not like) rats.
2 I (think) chameleons are OK.
3 My mum and dad (not want) a pet at home.
4 Tim (hate) cockroaches.
5 Redbacks (not live) in televisions.
6 A big spider (live) in our bathroom.
7 My sister and I (love) dogs.
8 Snakes (not make) good pets.

F

Write sentences about the animals you like and dislike.

Example: I don't like rats – they're absolutely revolting.

I love cats – they're really nice.

G

In pairs, tell your partner about your preferences.

Example: A: I love horses. They're fantastic.

B: Mmm, I think they're OK. I like dolphins. They're lovely.

H LONGMAN DICTIONARY SKILLS

The words underlined have more than one meaning. Look them up in the mini-dictionary and write the number of the appropriate meaning.

1 A lot of people are afraid of <u>bats</u>.
2 The ants are climbing up the <u>trunk</u> of that tree.
3 There is a big cockroach on the <u>floor</u>.
4 One of his <u>jobs</u> is to give food to the cats.
5 There is an interesting <u>article</u> about spiders in this magazine.

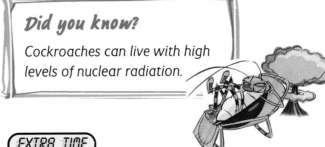

Did you know?

Cockroaches can live with high levels of nuclear radiation.

EXTRA TIME

Look at *World Club Magazine* on page 88.
Do activity 1.

2 Australian Animals

Fauna

The kangaroo has strong back legs, short front legs and a small head with long ears.

The koala is a marsupial with grey fur, a big black nose and long claws.

After thousands of years of isolation, Australia has some completely different groups of animals from other continents.

Firstly, there are marsupials like koalas and kangaroos. They are mammals but, after they are born, the babies live in their mother's pouch. The koala is a marsupial with grey fur, a big black nose and long claws. It lives in eucalyptus trees and eats the leaves.

The kangaroo has strong back legs, short front legs and a small head with long ears. The kangaroo lives in groups. It sleeps in the day and comes out at night to eat grass.

Another rare animal is the platypus. It is a mammal, but it lays eggs! The platypus has got a brown body, a long nose and sharp claws. It lives near rivers and eats small fish and insects.

A KEYWORDS

Match the words in the box with the numbers. Use the mini-dictionary to help you.

fur head ears nose body front legs
back legs claws eyes pouch

Example: fur 1

B

Read the text. Which is *your* favourite animal?

C

Read it again. Copy and complete the table.

	kangaroo	koala	platypus
habitat	all over Australia		
food	grass		
has got	strong back legs / small front legs		

Did you know?

A baby kangaroo stays in its mother's pouch for nine months after it is born.

D

Use the words to write sentences.

Example: 1 The koala is a marsupial **with** sharp claws, grey fur **and** a black nose.

1 koala / marsupial / sharp claws / grey fur / black nose
2 hippo / mammal / big body / small legs
3 ant / small insect / six legs / big head
4 penguin / bird / black and white body / small head
5 tiger / large cat / orange and black fur / sharp claws
6 elephant / very large mammal / grey body / big ears / a trunk

E

Choose an animal and write sentences about it.

Example:

Size/group: It is a large mammal.
Habitat: It lives in central and south Africa.
Food: It eats grass and leaves.
Abilities: It can run fast to escape lions.
Description: It is a horse with black and white stripes.

F

In groups, read your sentences. The other students guess your animal.

EXTRA TIME

Look at *World Club Magazine* on page 88. Do activity 2.

3 Quiz Time

A 🔑 KEYWORDS

Quiz. In pairs, match the animals with the habitats.

Example: trout – rivers

> **Animals:** trout / dolphin / tiger / camel / polar bear / puma
> **Habitats:** deserts / mountains / the sea / rivers / tropical forests / polar regions

B 📼

Listen to the quiz and look at the photos. Guess the animal.

C 📼

Listen again and answer the questions.

1 Where does it come from?
   a) Europe   b) Asia   c) Africa
2 Can it fly? a) yes   b) no
3 How big is it?
   a) 2 metres long   b) 1 metre long
   c) 3 metres long
4 What does it eat?
   a) leaves   b) meat   c) grass
5 What kind of animal is it?
   a) mammal   b) bird   c) insect
   d) reptile

Language Focus: Present Simple Questions

D

Copy and complete the table with these words.

main verb / question word / subject / auxiliary verb

QUESTIONS			
1 ...	2 ...	3 ...	4 ...
Where	do	I / you / we / they	live?
	does	he/she/it	
	Do	I / you / we / they	live in Asia?
	Does	he/she/it	

See Grammar Reference 2 on page 16.

E

Write questions and answer them.

Example: 1 Do bushbabies live in America?
No, they don't.

1 bushbabies / live / in America?
2 what / leopards / eat?
3 when / tigers / sleep?
4 komodo dragons / eat / grass?
5 where / redback spiders / live?

F

PRONUNCIATION: QUESTIONS
Listen to the questions.

Does it live in the desert?

Where does it live?

Listen and repeat.

G

In groups, one student thinks of an animal. The others can ask ten *yes/no* questions to find out what it is.

Example: A: Is it a mammal?
B: Yes, it is.

H

Work in pairs.

Student A: Look at page 108: Exercise 1.
Student B: Ask and answer questions to complete the table about the puma.

Example: What kind of animal is it?

Group/family	...
Continent	North and South America
Habitat	...
Size	up to 2.1 metres long
Colour	...
Food	meat ~ other animals, e.g. deer
Way of hunting	...
Other names	cougar, mountain lion

(EXTRA TIME)

Look at *World Club Magazine* on page 89.
Do activity 3.

Fluency

Writing: Brochure for a Zoo

A

Invent your own animal or choose a real animal.

Stage 1: Preparation

Find photos or draw your animal. Write notes about: name, category, description, habitat, food, abilities.

Example:

> Name: Koala
> Category: marsupial mammal
> Description:

Stage 2: Writing

Use your notes to write the description. Then check for mistakes.

Stage 3: Presentation

Produce a poster or short 'magazine'. Include your description, pictures and maps.

Write four questions for people to answer about your project.

Speaking: Finding Out

B

Find out about your partner's animal.

Stage 1: Preparation

Prepare questions in notes like this:

Example:

> name?
> mammal / reptile / bird?
> big or small?

Stage 2: Speaking

In pairs, ask and answer your questions.

Example: A: What's the name of your animal?
B: It's a platypus.
A: Is it a ...

Stage 3: Feedback

Give your partner's animal a score for interest.

3 very strange and exotic
2 quite interesting
1 not very interesting

Listening: 'The Ant and the Dove'

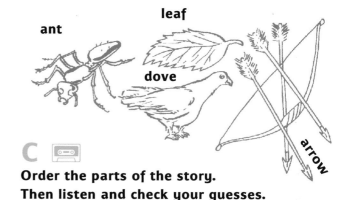

C

Order the parts of the story.
Then listen and check your guesses.

Example: b 1

a The ant climbs on the leaf.
b An ant falls into a river.
c The ant bites the man's leg.
d A dove sees the ant and drops a leaf in the water.
e 'Thank you, little ant,' says the dove.
f Later, a man sees the dove and decides to shoot her.
g The man jumps. His arrow misses the dove.

 **Consolidation**

Grammar

A

Put the verbs into the correct form.

Ostriches are enormous birds – two metres high. They (¹ live) on the plains of Africa. They can't fly but they (² move) very fast – 65 kph. They (³ not eat) insects, they (⁴ eat) small animals and plants. The female (⁵ lay) between six and eight eggs. Ostriches (⁶ not make) good pets.

B

Write questions about ostriches.

1 where / live?
2 what / eat?
3 eat / insects?
4 how many eggs / female lay?
5 make / good pets?

C

In pairs, imagine you are talking animals. Ask and answer questions about your lives.

What/name? Where/live? What/eat and drink? Where/sleep? What/do?

Example: A: Hi! My name's Rover. What's your name?
B: Ted. I'm a cocker spaniel and you?
A: I'm a rottweiler. Where...

Vocabulary

D KEYWORDS

Classify these animals:

> cobra   cockroach   koala   komodo dragon
> kangaroo   rat   ant   dove   ostrich   chameleon
> platypus   leopard   giant panda   penguin

M (mammal)   Mar (marsupial mammal)
R (reptile)   B (bird)   I (insect)

E

MEMORY GAME

• In groups, play this memory game:
A: At the zoo, there are ten penguins.
B: At the zoo, there are ten penguins and six elephants.
C: At the zoo, there are ten penguins, six elephants and ...

Pronunciation: /iː/ and /ɪ/ Sounds

F

Listen to these sounds then classify the words.

/iː/	/ɪ/
eat	it

Listen and check your answers.

sleep / live / eagle / chimpanzee / dolphin / listen / we / sea / insect / tree / platypus / leaf / she / meat

Module check

Grammar Reference

1 The present simple: affirmative and negative

	Affirmative	Negative
I/you/we/they	sing	don't sing
he/she/it	sings	doesn't sing

- The present simple is used to *express habitual actions*:

This bird **sings** beautifully. Lizards **love** the sun.
The eagle **doesn't sing**. Koalas **don't eat** meat.

- Remember! Verbs in the *third person singular* end with **s**: **he gives / she reads / it bites**
- Sometimes the ending of the verb changes a little: **he switches on / she goes / it flies**
- We use the auxiliaries **don't** and **doesn't** to form the *negative*:

He **doesn't like** snakes. Komodo dragons **don't** eat grass.

2 The present simple (interrogative)

Questions		
Do	I/you/we/they	play?
Does	he/she/it	play?

- To form the interrogative, we use **do** and **does**.

Do kangaroos **eat** grass?
Do they live in forests?

Yes, they **do**.
No, they **don't**.

Does the ostrich lay eggs?
Does it sing?

Yes, it **does**.
No, it **doesn't**.

What **does** the lion eat?
Where **do** zebras live?

Meat.
In Africa.

Keyword Check KEYWORDS

Animals (general): female, male, pet

Mammals: bat, bushbaby, giant panda, leopard, polar bear, puma, rat

Marsupials: kangaroo, koala, platypus

Fish: salmon, trout

Birds: eagle, ostrich, penguin

Reptiles: chameleon, komodo dragon, lizard, snake

Insects: ant, cockroach

Parts of body: legs, body, claw, fur, head, nose, pouch, wing

Adjectives: big, small, short, long, sharp

Habitats: desert, forest, mountain, polar region, river, sea

Food: fruit, grass, leaves, meat, nuts

Verbs: come out at night, drop, fall into a river, lay eggs, look for food, switch on the lights

Look through the module and add other important words to these lists.

1 Look at Grammar References 1 and 2 on this page and complete Grammar File 1 in the Activity Book. Then do the *Test Yourself: Grammar* on page 11 of the Activity Book.

2 Look at the Keyword Check. Write important new words in your vocabulary book. Then do the *Test Yourself: Vocabulary* on page 11 of the Activity Book.

HOMES

Lead-in

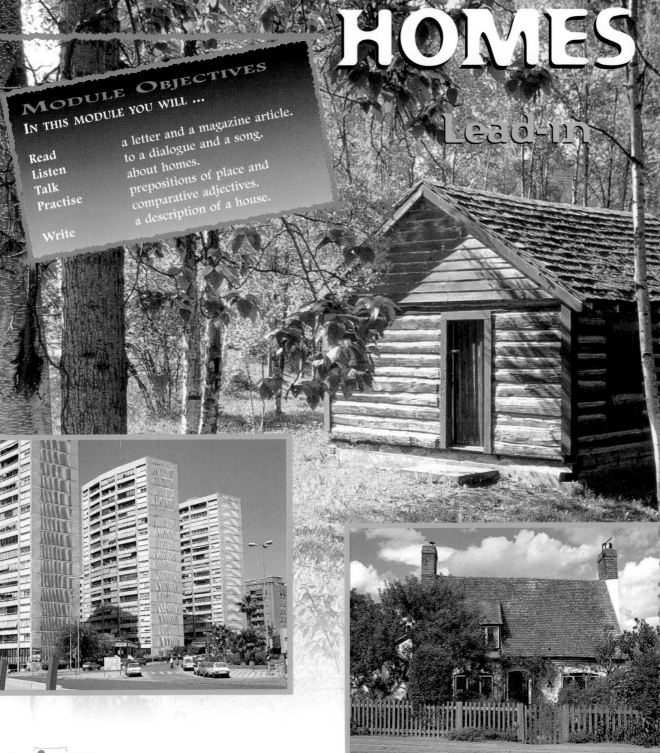

MODULE OBJECTIVES

IN THIS MODULE YOU WILL ...

Read   a letter and a magazine article.
Listen   to a dialogue and a song.
Talk   about homes.
Practise   prepositions of place and
       comparative adjectives.
Write   a description of a house.

---

a KEYWORDS

Look at the words in the box. Identify the three kinds of homes in the photos. Use the mini-dictionary to help you.

> igloo   tent   log cabin   block of flats
> country cottage   mansion   terraced house

b

Tell your partner about your home. Use these ideas: bedrooms, garden, balcony, floors.

Example: A: I live in a flat in a town. The block has got five floors. My flat has got six...

4 Village Houses

A KEYWORDS

Match the words in the box with the drawings.

passage   bathroom   living room
bedroom   hall   kitchen   cellar   stairs

Language Focus: Prepositions

B 🔲

Listen to the dialogue. Which of the houses in the photos is the travel agent describing?

C 🔲

Listen again and complete these sentences.

above / on the left / between / on / in front of / behind / next to / in / under / on the right

1 It's ... a small village ... the coast.
2 ... there's a big kitchen and ... there's a large living room. Ah, and ... the kitchen there's a small cellar.
3 The main bedroom is ... the living room and ... the main bedroom, there's a wooden balcony.
4 There's a small garden ... the house.
5 It's ... the village shop and the bar, but ... of the house there are fields.

See Grammar Reference 3 on page 26.

18

D

Match the prepositions from exercise C with these pictures.

E

Choose the correct preposition.

1 My flat is a) *in* b) *on* the tenth floor.

2 We live a) *under* b) *above* my grandparents – they're on the ninth floor.

3 When you come into the flat, the kitchen is a) *in front of* b) *behind* you.

4 There is a small table a) *in* b) *on* the kitchen – where we have breakfast.

5 The bathroom is a) *next* b) *between* the kitchen and the living room.

6 My room is a) *next to* b) *between* my sister Ana's room.

F

Draw a simple plan and write sentences describing a flat.

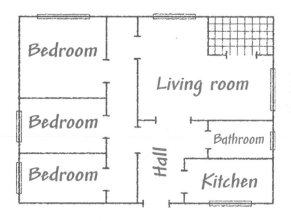

Example:

There is a long hall. The living room is on the right. The kitchen is in front of...

G

In pairs, describe your flat to your partner. Your partner draws the plan.

H

DICTIONARY SKILLS

Circle the correct word. Use the mini-dictionary.

1 Cockroaches usually *appear / appearance* at night.

2 I like to *sing / song* in the bathroom.

3 *Explores / Explorers* talk about strange animals.

4 He isn't *adventure / adventurous*. He stays at home.

(EXTRA TIME)

Look at *World Club Magazine* on page 89. Do activity 4.

5 My Room

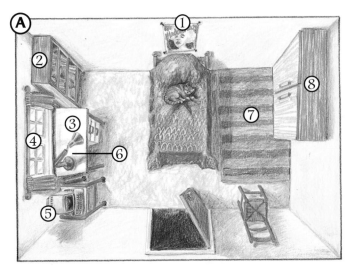

A 🔑 KEYWORDS

Match the words with the numbers in picture A.

> lamp wardrobe desk carpet
> bookshelves poster curtains
> personal computer

B 💬

In pairs, find eight differences between the two pictures.

Example: A: 'In picture A the lamp is on the desk. In picture B it is on the bookshelves'.

C

Look at the photo. Give the room a score.

1 not very interesting or comfortable
2 quite attractive – a nice place to be
3 fantastic – a really great place

D

Read the letter. What can you guess about the person?

1 He is a) seven b) ten c) fourteen.
2 He is very interested in a) music b) sport c) films.
3 He a) likes b) doesn't like collecting things.
4 He is a) a very practical b) not a very practical person.
5 Now he a) plays b) doesn't play the guitar.

36 Keswick Avenue,
Bristol BR2 8NR,

Dear Marek,

How are you? Thanks for your letter.

You want me to describe my house. Well, it's very different from yours. It's a flat on the ninth floor.

My favourite room is my bedroom. I spend a lot of time there. The walls are blue and grey (I painted them!) – and there are lots of posters. I collect signed posters of rock groups at concerts – my favourite is one of Portishead.

My bed is on the left and there's a wardrobe for clothes on the right. My desk is in front of the window and I've got lots of plants on it. I've also got a computer (mum's old one!). I only use it sometimes for games and to do projects for school.

In the corner, I've got some shelves for my books and CD's. I've got my collection of rocks and fossils there too. I collect them when we go on holiday to the coast.

I don't like throwing things away. Under my bed I've got lots of old things I don't use now – my guitar, toys, a football...

E

Look at two ways of expressing addition.

I've got lots of plants on it. I've *also* got a computer.

I've got my collection of rocks and fossils there *too.*

Complete the sentences with too or *also*.

1 I've got a CD player in my room. I've ... got a cassette player.
2 On my desk there's a photo of my dog. There's a photo of my boyfriend ...
3 You can see the river from my window. You can ... see the mountains.
4 My sister's got a canary in her room. She's got two goldfish ...

F

In pairs, find out about your partner's bedroom. Ask about:

- size
- colour of walls/pictures and posters on walls
- position of doors, windows and furniture
- important personal possessions

Example: A: How big is your room?

B: It is quite small.

(EXTRA TIME)

Look at *World Club Magazine* on page 90. Do activity 5.

Homes

21

6 Unusual Homes

Unusual Homes

1 The idea of living in a lighthouse is romantic, but there are some problems. First, all the rooms are round so it is more difficult to find furniture! Lighthouses are also more isolated than other houses. That's fine if you want a quieter life, but visiting friends is not easy.

2 Eco-houses look stranger than other houses, but they are more ecological. The materials conserve heat and absorb solar energy. In one of the walls there are tanks full of water, which the sun heats up. Eco-houses are also more economical than normal houses there are no gas or electricity bills to pay.

3 London doubledecker buses make practical homes. They are better than most buses, because they are bigger and have two floors. Doubledeckers are noisier than other mobile homes, but they are more convenient. When you get tired of a place, you can just start up the engine and move somewhere else.

A KEYWORDS

Match these adjectives with the houses in the photos.

> romantic isolated quiet practical noisy
> convenient strange ecological economical

B

Listen to and read the magazine article. Check your guesses from exercise A.

C

Read the article again and list the advantages and disadvantages of living in each house.

Example: Lighthouse – advantage= romantic/quiet

Language Focus: Comparatives

D

Find adjectives in the text to match the categories below.

Example: bigger 1

COMPARATIVES	
1 Short adjectives + 'er' *	small – small**er** (**than**)
2 Long adjectives + more/less	interesting – **more** interesting (**than**)
3 Irregular adjectives – complete change	bad – **worse** (**than**)

* Spelling differences: large = larg**er**
easy = eas**ier**   hot = hot**ter**

See Grammar Reference 4 on page 26.

E

Use these words to write sentences.

Example: 1 Eco-houses are more ecological than lighthouses.

1 eco-houses / ecological / lighthouses
2 lighthouses / quiet / doubledecker buses
3 doubledecker buses / convenient / lighthouses
4 eco-houses / small / lighthouses
5 doubledecker buses / ecological / eco-houses

F

PRONUNCIATION: /ə/ SOUND

Listen to the pronunciation of these words in a sentence:

noisi*er than*

Doubledeckers are noisi*er than* mobile homes.

Listen and repeat the sentences.

G

Work in pairs.

Student A: Look at page 108: Exercise 2.

Student B: Ask and answer questions to find six differences between your picture and your partner's picture.

Example: In my picture there is a small table under the window. Is there a table in your picture?

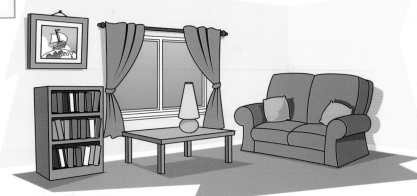

 EXTRA TIME

Look at *World Club Magazine* on page 90.
Do activity 6.

Fluency

Writing: Describing Houses

A

Invent an unusual house and describe it.

Stage 1: Preparation

Draw a plan and a drawing of a house.

Write notes about it:

location – in the forest

appearance – in a tree, 2 windows, 1 door

rooms – kitchen, bathroom, living room, bedroom

furniture – big table, sofa, piano, beds

machines – 2 televisions, computer, lift

Stage 2: Writing/Checking

Use your notes to write a description.

Give your description to your partner to correct the mistakes.

Write a final version of your description.

Speaking: True/False Quiz

B

Stage 1: Preparation

In groups of four, read the descriptions from exercise A. Individually, write true and false sentences about the houses.

Example: Ahmet's house is in the forest. (true)
In Blanca's house there are three lifts. (false)

Stage 2: Speaking

Take turns to say the sentences. The others guess if they are true or false.

Example: Blanca: There are two bedrooms in Ahmet's house.
Stefan: True.
Blanca: No, false. There are three!

Stage 3: Reporting

Tell the class about your houses.

Example: Blanca's house is very modern. It's got...

Listening: A Song

C

Listen to the song and complete the chorus.

Sweet [1] ... Alabama.
[2] ... the skies [3] ...   so [4] ...
Sweet [5] ... Alabama.
Lord, [6] ... coming [7]...   to [8] ...

Consolidation

Grammar

A

Complete these sentences about the island with these words:

on / left / behind / next to / right

1 There is a small garden ... the cottage.
2 ... the cave there are two palm trees.
3 On the ... of the island there is a cave.
4 On the ... of the island there is a windmill.
5 The lighthouse is ... a rock ... the sea.

B

TREASURE HUNT

• In pairs, one person thinks of a place on the map to hide some treasure.
• The other asks questions to find out where it is.

Example: A: Is it under the big tree?
　　　　　B: No it isn't.

C

Write five sentences comparing your home with the houses on the map.

Example: My flat is bigger than the cottage.

small / big	quiet / noisy
expensive / economical	romantic / practical
modern / old	comfortable / uncomfortable

Vocabulary

D KEYWORDS

Classifly these words:

carpet / kitchen / igloo / flat / curtains / hall / wardrobe / desk / cottage / bookshelves / terraced house / living room / cellar / storeroom / lamp

Houses	Furniture	Rooms
igloo	carpet	kitchen

Pronunciation: Word Stress

E

Listen to these words:

□□	□□□	□□□
kitchen	piano	balcony

Copy and classify these words:

kitchen / piano / balcony / romantic / beautiful / cottage / description / village / collection / mansion / bedroom / furniture / location / practical / comfortable

Listen and check your answers. Listen again and repeat the words.

Module check

Grammar Reference

3 Prepositions

- Prepositions are used to *connect* words in a sentence.
- This module presents prepositions of **place**. They indicate the **position** of people, buildings, objects, etc:

above our flat / **under** the bed
on the left / **right** of the living room
in front of / **behind** the house
next to the church / **in** the garden
on the first floor

4 Comparatives

- Adjectives can be **short**, **long** or **irregular**.
- **Short:** 1 syllable, or 2 syllables that end in *y*:

adjective	*comparative*
short	short**er**
big	big**ger**
easy	eas**ier**

- For adjectives ending in **consonant~vowel~consonant** (e.g. big, hot, red), **the final consonant is doubled**. One exception: **w** (already double).

- For adjectives ending in **y**, the **y** changes to **i** when the preceding letter is a **consonant** (e.g. hea**vy**).

- **Long:** 2 syllables that do not end in *y*, or more than 2 syllables:

adjective	*comparative*
romantic	**more** romantic / **less** romantic

- **Irregular:** they change completely:

adjective	*comparative*
good / bad	**better** / **worse**

- To compare two elements, we use the comparative form of the adjective and the word **than**:

A flat is **cheaper than** a mansion.
A lighthouse is **more romantic than** a mobile home.

Keyword Check

Houses: cottage, flat, lighthouse, mansion, tent, terraced house

General: balcony, downstairs, floor, stairs, terrace, upstairs, wall, window

Rooms: bathroom, bedroom, cellar, hall, kitchen, living room

Furniture: bed, bookshelves, cupboard, curtains, desk, piano, poster

Machines: CD player, television, computer, lift

Adjectives: attractive, ecological, large, modern, noisy, quiet, romantic, strange

Verbs: come into (enter), get tired of (something), go up/down (stairs), throw away (old things)

Look through the module and add other important words to these lists.

1 **Look at Grammar References 3 and 4 on this page and complete Grammar File 2 in the Activity Book. Then do the *Test Yourself: Grammar* on page 18 of the Activity Book.**

2 **Look at the Keyword Check. Write important new words in your vocabulary book. Then do the *Test Yourself: Vocabulary* on page 18 of the Activity Book.**

Homes

STORIES

Lead-in

Module Objectives

In this module you will ...

Read	a TV film guide and a picture story.
Listen	to a story and a quiz.
Talk	about films and books.
Write	about a film.
Practise	adverbs of frequency and the present continuous tense.

a KEYWORDS

Match the words in the box with the films and books (1–5). Use the mini-dictionary.

THE MOSQUITO COAST
PAUL THEROUX
PENGUIN READERS
Bram Stoker
PENGUIN READERS
CHANDLER
THE LAKE
PENGUIN READERS

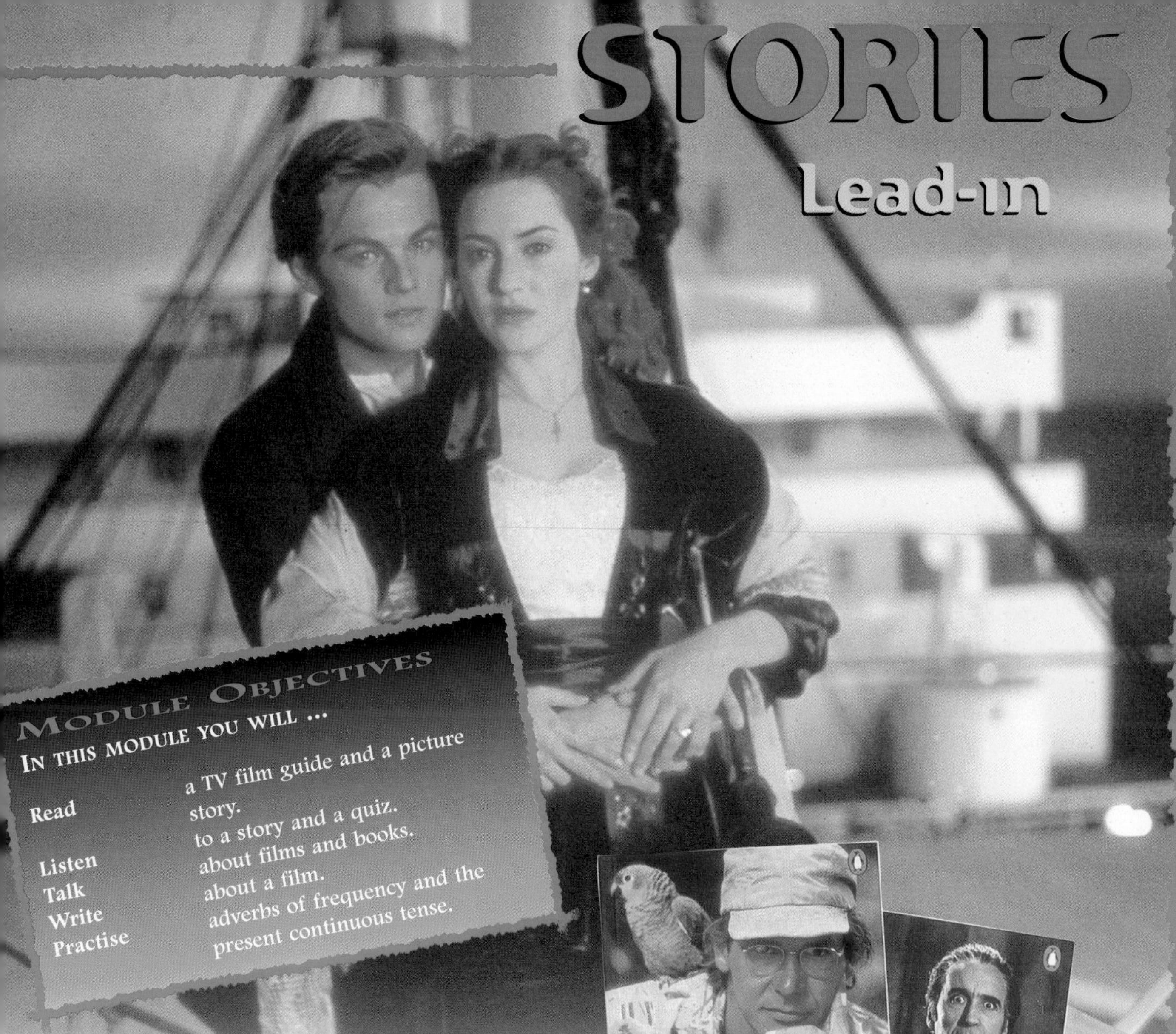

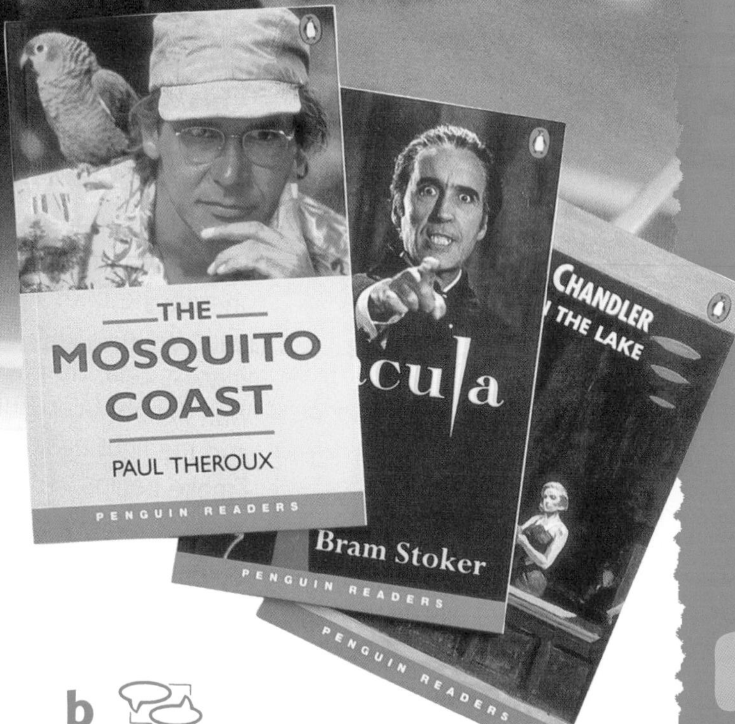

> horror romantic science fiction comedy adventure historical fantasy

Example: Titanic – romantic, historical

1. *Titanic*
2. *Indiana Jones and the Last Crusade*
3. *Dracula*
4. *Bean – the Ultimate Disaster Movie*
5. *Alien*

b

What are your favourite films and books? Tell the class.

Example: My favourite film is *Jurassic Park.* My favourite book is *The Hobbit.*

7 Films

Princess Leia and R2-D2

Darth Vader

TV-1

Here is another chance to see this classic science fiction film.

FILM NIGHT: BBC 1, 9.00 p.m.   STAR WARS (1977) Director: George Lucas

In another galaxy, the evil Empire controls nearly everybody – except the 'Rebels'.

The story begins when the rebel Princess Leia (Carrie Fisher) finds plans for the 'Death Star', a terrible weapon. She hides the plans in a robot, R2-D2, with the message: 'Help me, Obi-Wan Kenobi. You're my only hope.' R2-D2 escapes to the planet Tattooine with another robot, C-3PO.

The hero, Luke Skywalker (Mark Hamill), lives on Tattooine on his uncle's farm. He often dreams of a more exciting life. One day he finds R2-D2 and reads the message from Princess Leia. He goes to Obi-Wan Kenobi (Alec Guinness) and the fight against the Empire begins.

There is rarely a boring moment in the film. It is sometimes very funny – the two robots usually argue about everything! Darth Vader is a memorable villain – we never see his face behind the black mask. And, of course, the special effects are always brilliant. In fact, in many ways...

A 🔑 KEYWORDS

Read the text quickly and find the names of these characters.

> the princess   the two robots
> the hero   the villain

B 📖

Read the text carefully and choose the correct answer.

1 The 'Death Star' can a) help people b) destroy people c) hide people

2 Luke's life is a) exciting b) boring c) easy

3 Luke fights a) Obi-Wan Kenobi b) the Empire c) the robots

4 The film is a) boring but funny b) exciting and funny c) boring but memorable

C   KEYWORDS

Match these words from the text with the definitions.

1	terrible	a	not boring
2	exciting	b	amusing
3	boring	c	very bad
4	funny	d	very good
5	memorable	e	uninteresting
6	brilliant	f	easy to remember

Language Focus: Adverbs of Frequency

D

Find these words in the text. Then copy and complete the chart.

often / rarely / sometimes / usually / never / always

100% always
    80% ...
        60% ...
            30% ...
                5% ...
                    0% ...

E

Look at the adverbs in the text again. Complete these rules with _before_ or _after_.

> Adverbs of frequency go [1] ... the verb 'to be'.
> Adverbs of frequency go [2] ... other verbs.

See Grammar Reference 5 on page 36.

F

Write sentences using the words.

Example: 1 The film is sometimes very funny.

1 very funny / sometimes / is / the film
2 wears / Darth Vader / a black mask / always
3 there are / in the film / often / exciting fights
4 never / the Empire / good things / does
5 agree / the two robots / rarely
6 in the end / wins / the hero / always

G

Think about your answers for this questionnaire. Then, in pairs, tell your partner.

Example: A: I often go to the cinema with my friends.

B: I don't. I always go with my parents.

> ○ ## DO YOU EVER ...
> ○
> ○ • _go to the cinema with your friends?_
>   • _cry during romantic films?_
> ○ • _watch videos in English?_
>   • _close your eyes during horror films?_
> ○ • _laugh loudly during comedy films?_

H LONGMAN DICTIONARY SKILLS

Are these words nouns, verbs, adjectives, adverbs or prepositions? Put them into the correct category and then check your answers in the mini-dictionary.

noisy finally living room then
throw away before romantic next to

(EXTRA TIME)

Look at _World Club Magazine_ on page 90. Do activity 7.

KING MIDAS AND THE GOLDEN TOUCH

Stories

A After that, he touches his food and it changes into gold!

B One day, Midas sees an old man in his garden.

C When he touches his daughter, she turns into gold.

D Finally, he swims in a river and the 'golden touch' disappears.

E Then, he takes the old man to the god, Dionysus, and makes a wish.

A KEYWORDS

Find these things in the pictures.

> a palace   an old man   a Greek god   a king
> food   trees   flowers   a golden statue

B

Read the title and captions and put the pictures in the correct order. Then listen to the story and check your answers.

C

Listen again. What things does Midas change into gold?

Example: a door, a table …

D

PRONUNCIATION: CONTRACTIONS
Listen to the sentences from the story. Count the words.

Example: 1 He's rich. = 3 words

E

Use these notes and the mini-dictionary to write the story of Perseus and Medusa.

Example: One day, a god changes Medusa into…

> **Perseus and Medusa**
>
> one day / a god / change Medusa into a monster / has got snakes for hair / big wings
>
> when / she / look at people / they / change into statues / many men / try to kill her
>
> then / Perseus / go to the cave
>
> Medusa / see her reflection in his shield / after that / she / change into statue
>
> finally / Perseus / cut off her head

F

Do you know any other myths or legends? Tell the class.

Example: El Cid, King Arthur, Hercules, …

 EXTRA TIME

Look at *World Club Magazine* on page 91. Do activity 8.

31

9 A Picture Story

A KEYWORDS

Read the story. Are these sentences true or false. Use the mini-dictionary.

1 Kathy is **confident** at first.
2 Danny can't go to the party because he is **ill**.

3 Danny is a **shy** person.
4 Kathy is **disappointed** after the phone call.
5 Kathy's friend is not very **helpful**.

Language Focus 1: Present Continuous

B

Copy and complete the tables.

AFFIRMATIVE			
I		[1] ...	
you / we / they		**are**	study**ing**.
he / she / it		[2] ...	

NEGATIVE			
I		**am not**	
you / we / they		[3] ...	feel**ing** very well.
he / she / it		[4] ...	

QUESTIONS			
What	[5] ...	you	do**ing**?
Why	[6] ...	she	feel**ing** depressed?
	Is	he	danc**ing**?
	[7] ...	they	talk**ing**?

See Grammar Reference 6 on page 36.

C

Complete the story with the verbs in the present continuous.

Example: 1 are talking

When the story begins, Kathy and Danny [1] ... (talk) on the phone. Danny says he can't go to the party. He [2] ... (not study) for his science test – that is just an excuse. Danny's mother [3] ... (listen) to them! 'You [4] ... (not do) your homework,' she says. 'Go to the party!'

Kathy and her friend go to the party. Some people [5] ... (dance), others [6] ... (eat) and drinking. They are happy when they see Danny. He [7] ... (stand) in the corner, alone.

Language Focus 2: Present Continuous vs. Present Simple

D

Look at the example sentences and complete the rules.

Present continuous	Present simple
He can't answer the phone – he *is having* a shower.	He *has* a shower every morning.
We *are studying* English at the moment.	We *study* English three times a week.

We use the [1] ... for activities happening at the moment.

We use the [2] ... for habits and routines.

See Grammar Reference 6 again on page 36.

E

Choose the correct verb.

Example: 1 does

1 She *does/is doing* her homework every night.
2 She can't come to the phone – she *does/is doing* her homework.
3 Oh, no! It *rains/is raining*.
4 It often *rains/is raining* in England.
5 Pablo always *sits/is sitting* near me.
6 At the moment Pablo *sits/is sitting* with Oscar.

(EXTRA TIME)

Look at *World Club Magazine* on page 91. Do activity 9.

Stories

Fluency

Writing: A Story

A

Write the story of a film or book you know well.

Stage 1: Preparation

Write notes in a time-line.
Example:

> ### Anne in New York
> • Anne leaves home
> • Jim meets 'Mr Big' at the airport
> • Jim gives him some money

Stage 2: Writing

Write the story in three parts:

1 What is happening at the beginning.

One day, Jim is looking out of the window. It is raining. He sees his girlfriend, Anne. She is getting into a car.

2 What happens – the basic story.

Jim goes to the airport. He meets 'Mr Big'.

3 What happens in the end.

Finally, Jim finds Anne and...

Stage 3: Checking

Check your work for:
- punctuation, spelling and verb tenses
- linking words (*one day, then, when, after that, finally,* etc.)

Speaking: Reading Survey

B

Do a class survey on reading habits.

Stage 1: Preparation

In groups, write three questions for the survey. Everybody copies them.
Example: How often do you read magazines?
   a) often **b)** sometimes **c)** never

Stage 2: Speaking

Form new groups. Take turns to ask your questions and write the results.

Stage 3: Display

Draw a bar graph for each question to show the results. Tell the class about it.

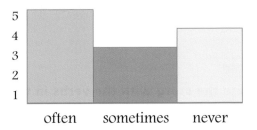

Reading Magazines

Listening: A Quiz

C

What can you remember about the stories in this module? Listen and choose the answer – a, b or c.

 # Consolidation

Grammar

A

Put the adverb in the correct position.

1 They go to the cinema. (often)
2 Photo stories are funny. (sometimes)
3 I read before I go to sleep. (usually)
4 Roald Dahl's books are interesting. (always)
5 He reads romantic stories. (never)

B

Complete the sentences with the present continuous tense.

1 A: What ... (happen) at the start of the story?
  B: The hero ... (drive) his car.
2 A: ... he ... (pay) attention?
  B: No. He ... (not drive) very well. He ... (talk) on his mobile phone.
3 A: Why does the accident happen?
  B: Two girls ... (cross) the road, but they... (not look) where they ... (go).
4 A: What is the weather like?
  B: It ... (rain).

C

Choose the correct verb for each sentence.

1 I *clean/am cleaning* my dad's car every Saturday.
2 It *rains/is raining* at the moment.
3 My mother *meets/is meeting* me after school every day.
4 I always *go/am going* to school by bus.
5 Listen! What *does he say/is he saying*?
6 Mary usually *does/is doing* her homework well.

Vocabulary

D   KEYWORDS

Complete the film review with the words in the box.

> effects romantic exciting villain characters boring historical

Titanic is a ¹ ... and ² ... film. The two main ³ ... are Rose (Kate Winslet) and Jack (Leonardo DiCaprio). There isn't a ⁴ ... in the story – except maybe the iceberg! The special ⁵ ... are brilliant. I thought it was a really ⁶ ... film, but the beginning was a bit ⁷...

E  KEYWORDS

Match the words with the definitions.

a a palace
b a villain
c confident
d sometimes
e a princess
f a comedy

1 a funny film
2 not often
3 where a King lives
4 not shy
5 a bad person
6 a King's daughter

Pronunciation: Word Stress

F

Listen to the words and classify them.

▫◼▫	◼▫▫
romantic	comedy

romantic / comedy / exciting / character / adventure / fantasy / confident / memorable / amusing

Module check

Grammar Reference

5 Adverbs of frequency

• Adverbs of frequency are used to indicate **how often** we do something:

always	100 % of the time	sometimes	30 % of the time
often	80 % of the time	rarely	5 % of the time
usually	60 % of the time	never	0 % of the time

• Position of the adverbs:

Before the main verb:

The hero **rarely** loses.

After the verb *to be*:

The villain is **always** a very bad person.

6 Present continuous: affirmative, negative and interrogative

	Affirmative	Negative	Questions		
I he she it	am talking is talking	am not talking is not talking (isn't talking)	Am Is	I he she it	talking? talking?
you we they	are talking	are not talking (aren't talking)	Are	you we they	talking?

Are they going to the party?　Yes, they **are**.

Is Miguel waiting for us?　No, he **isn't**.

What **are** they drinking?　They're **drinking** cola.

Where **is** he going now?　He's **going** to the cinema.

• We use the present continuous to talk about actions taking place now:

Maribel **is dancing** with Pere.

The friends **are having** pizza and a cola.

It **is** not **raining**.

Keyword Check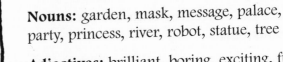

Stories: adventure, comedy, fantasy, historical, horror, photo story, romantic, science fiction

Nouns: garden, mask, message, palace, party, princess, river, robot, statue, tree

Adjectives: brilliant, boring, exciting, funny, ill, memorable, old, terrible

Character: confident, disappointed, helpful, sad, shy

Films: characters, hero, special effects, villain

Sequence: one day, then, next, when, after that, finally

Look through the module and add other important words to these lists.

1 **Look at Grammar References 5 and 6 on this page and complete Grammar File 3 in the Activity Book. Then do the *Test Yourself: Grammar* on page 25 of the Activity Book.**

2 **Look at the Keyword Check. Write important new words in your vocabulary book. Then do the *Test Yourself: Vocabulary* on page 25 of the Activity Book.**

MODULE OBJECTIVES

IN THIS MODULE YOU WILL …

Read	an Internet page, song lyrics and a magazine interview.
Listen	to songs.
Talk	about film stars, pop stars and sports stars.
Write	about a star.
Practise	the past simple tense.

a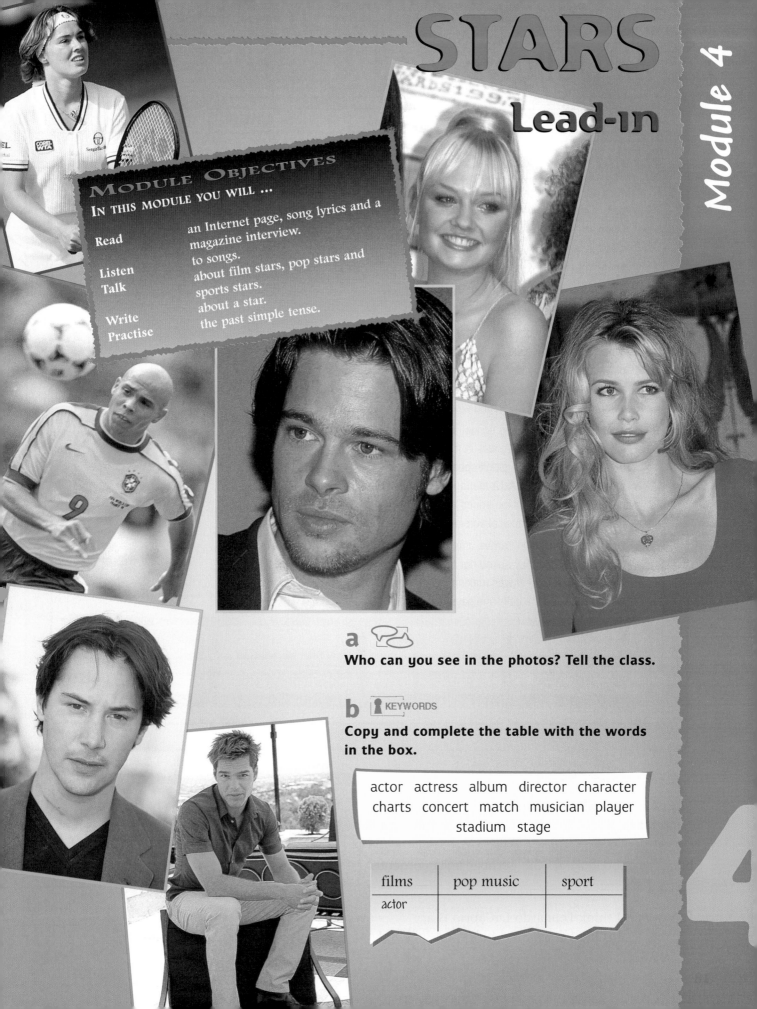

Who can you see in the photos? Tell the class.

b KEYWORDS

Copy and complete the table with the words in the box.

> actor actress album director character
> charts concert match musician player
> stadium stage

films	pop music	sport
actor		

4

10 Hollywood

Worldwide Hollywood Website

Back | Forward | Stop | Home | Refresh | Search | Favourites | Print | Font | Mail

1 Kate Winslet was born in Reading, England, on 5th October, 1975, so she is a 'Libra'.

2 She has got blue eyes, and her natural hair colour is blond. She has got 'Titanic' feet – size 44!

3 Classical music, Indigo Girls, Portishead, Oasis, Crowded House.

4 There is a history of acting in the Winslet family. When Kate was a child, her grandparents presented plays and musicals in their garden! Both her parents act, and her two sisters are actresses, so it was no surprise when Kate entered the acting profession.

5 Kate started at an acting school, but she didn't like it. Her first job (aged 12) was in a TV advert for a breakfast cereal – she didn't speak, but danced with the 'Honey Monster'! As a teenager, she acted small parts in various television series and also played the part of Wendy in a musical version of Peter Pan.

6 Her first big part didn't arrive until Heavenly Creatures. When they asked her to be the star, she had a job in a bar – 'I was making sandwiches when I received the call!' she says.

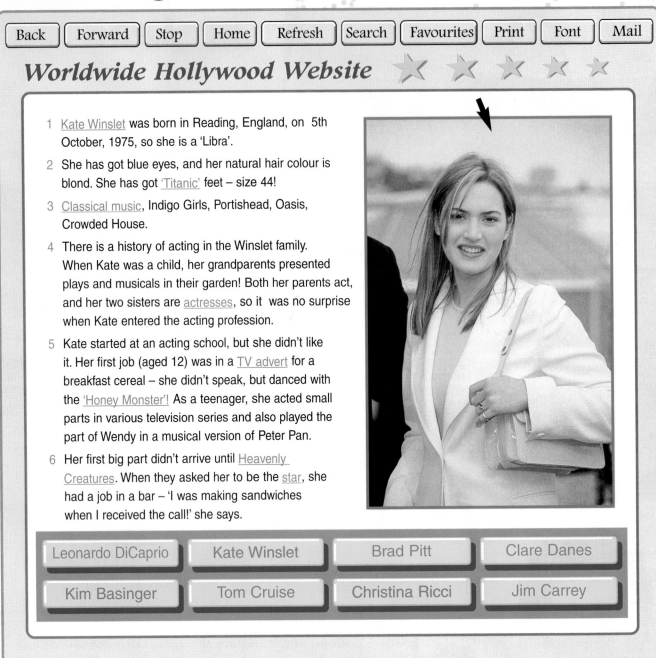

| Leonardo DiCaprio | Kate Winslet | Brad Pitt | Clare Danes |
| Kim Basinger | Tom Cruise | Christina Ricci | Jim Carrey |

A KEYWORDS

In pairs, talk about your favourite actors and actresses.

brilliant good-looking OK terrible ugly gorgeous

Example: I think Leonardo DiCaprio is a brilliant actor. And he's good-looking!

B

Read the text and match these titles with the paragraphs.

Family / Favourite Music / Birthday / Appearance /Big Break / Early Experience

Example: 1 Birthday

C

Are these sentences true or false?

1 Kate Winslet is American.
2 She has got large feet.
3 She doesn't like classical music.
4 She comes from an acting family.
5 Kate enjoyed acting school.
6 Her first big part was Wendy in *Peter Pan*.

Language Focus: Past Simple (Regular)

D LEARN TO LEARN

Look at the verbs in the boxes.

AFFIRMATIVE
Kate **started** at an acting school.

NEGATIVE
She **didn't like** it.

How do regular verbs end in the affirmative? How do we form negatives? Find more examples in the text.

See Grammar Reference 7 on page 46.

E LONGMAN DICTIONARY SKILLS

Are these words correctly spelled? Use the mini-dictionary.

directer   fruit   balconey   science
characther   dissappointed   palase
exciting   terible   kichen

Hollywood Factfile

- The world's first cinema [1] ... (open) in Paris in 1895 – but only 35 people [2] ... (arrive) at the first show!
- Walt Disney [3] ... (not invent) Mickey Mouse – it was his friend, Ub Iwerks. In 1928, Mickey Mouse [4] ... (receive) more letters than any other Hollywood star!
- T.C. Mapother IV is a famous film star. He [5] ... (change) his name, of course – to Tom Cruise!
- Most people [6] ... (not notice), but the dog that [7] ... (play) 'Lassie' was male!
- Jack Nicholson [8] ... (earn) $25 million for his part in Batman!
- Harrison Ford [9] ... (star) in three Indiana Jones films.
- In Jurassic Park (1993), they [10] ... (use) computers for the special effects of the dinosaurs.

Stars

F

Copy and complete the sentences with the past simple tense.

Example: 1 opened

G

CINEMA QUIZ

- In pairs, think of five things you know about film stars. Then, test another pair.

Example: A: She starred in the *Alien* films.
       B: Sigourney Weaver?
       A: Correct.

 EXTRA TIME

Look at *World Club Magazine* on page 91. Do activity 10.

Pop Stars

A   KEYWORDS

Tell the class about your favourite pop stars. Use the words in the box.

> album group musician singer song

Example: My favourite album is *Talk On Corners* by *The Corrs*.

B

Read the song. Then listen to find the missing words.

AIR GUITAR *

When I was just a kid like [1] ...
I did the moonwalk and the breakdance too.
But the thing that was best by far
Was when I [2] ... that air guitar.

Air guitar, it makes you feel like a big rock [3] ...
You can do it in the kitchen,
you can do it in the [4] ...
Keep on playing that air guitar.

I see that rock star on [5] ...
He's playing his guitar just like me.
He sings about freedom and justice too.
When I grow up I want to do that [6] ...

When it's raining and there's nothing to [7] ... Don't sit around feeling
blue. Remember this
song that I'm singing to [8] ...
Play air guitar,
make faces too.

* 'air guitar' =
imaginary guitar

Stars

AQUA

THE CORRS

BACKSTREET BOYS

40

C

In the song, find:

1 the names of two dances
2 two places you can play 'air guitar'
3 two things to sing about
4 two things to do on a rainy day

D

Match these words from the song with the definitions.

1	kid	a	liberty
2	keep on	b	young person
3	freedom	c	get older
4	grow up	d	sad
5	blue	e	continue

E

Complete the text with *and*, *but* or *because*.

Gloria wanted to be a pop star [1] ... she didn't know how to play an instrument. She learned how to play the guitar [2] ... formed a group. They were quite popular locally [3] ... they played lots of small concerts, [4] ... they didn't earn much money. Then they met *The Corrs* [5] ... toured with them, [6] ... only for one summer. Finally, Gloria decided to leave the group [7] ... she wanted to go solo.

F

PRONUNCIATION: 'ed' ENDINGS
Classify these words.

liked / played / acted / danced / started / changed / enjoyed / looked / presented / decided / toured / walked

/ d /	/ t /	/ ɪd / *
play**ed**	lik**ed**	act**ed**

*This ending adds an extra syllable to the word.

Now listen and check your answers.

G

In pairs, write two lines of a song. Think of words that rhyme.

Examples: kid / did; blue / do / you;
fight / night / right; day / say / way;
be / free / me; cry / try / why

Write the lines and show them to another pair. Read the best ones to the class.

Example: Every time I'm feeling blue,
I always try to think of you.

EXTRA TIME

Look at *World Club Magazine* on page 92.
Do activity 11.

Stars

41

12 Sporting Greats

A 🔑 KEYWORDS

Match the names with the sports in the box.

Mika Hakkinen / Miguel Indurain /
Michael Owen / Arantxa Sánchez Vicario /
Severiano Ballesteros

> cycling golf football motor racing tennis

Add more stars to the list.

Stars

STAR INTERVIEW

**Arantxa –
the Barcelona
Bumblebee**

Arantxa Sánchez Vicario is one of the top women tennis players in the world. We interviewed her tennis coach last week.

1?

I don't know! An American journalist, Bud Collins, first called her that.

2?

I think she started when she was four years old. She copied her brothers. She also liked to take her racket to dinner with her! She called it her 'best friend'.

3?

Yes, just before her fourteenth birthday.

4?

No, they didn't. She wanted to be a tennis player from the moment she picked up a racket.

5?

Absolutely great! I think she jumped over the net!

One final question. 6?

Well, someone presented her with these two beautiful dogs, Yorkshire terriers, after her victory in the Roland Garros tournament in Paris in 1989. Roland often travels with her – he brings her good luck!

B

Read the interview and match these questions with the gaps.

Example: 1 d

a Did she play as a professional at an early age?

b When did she start playing tennis?

c Why did she call her dogs 'Roland' and 'Garros?

d Why did they call her 'The Barcelona Bumblebee'?

e Did her parents force her to play tennis?

f How did she react after her first big victory?

Language Focus: Past Simple Questions

C

Copy and complete with these words:

subject / question word / main verb / auxiliary verb

1 ...	2 ...	3 ...	4 ...
When	did	she	start...
	Did	her parents	force...

See Grammar Reference 8 on page 46.

D

Write questions using the cues.

1 when / you start playing?

2 why / you like your sport?

3 your parents want you to get a job?

4 when / you reach your first final?

5 you receive a lot of money?

6 how / you celebrate?

E

Write questions for these answers.

Example: 1 What team did he join?

1 He joined Juventus. (What team)

2 She learned to play chess when she was three. (When)

3 Yes, they enjoyed the match. (Did)

4 I started because my parents played tennis. (Why)

5 No, she didn't dance in the final. (Did)

F

Work in pairs.

Student A: Look at page 108: Exercise 3.

Student B: Ask your partner questions to complete the passage about the great footballer, Pele.

Example: 1 When was he born?

Edson Arantes do Nascimento was born in Brazil in .... (1 *When?*). His friends called him Pele. He was very good at football. He was only ..... (2 *How old?*) when he played for the national team. He scored two goals in .... (3 *When?*), the following year, to help Brazil win the World Cup. He played ..... (4 *How many?*) games for his team, Santos, and scored 1216 goals. Then he joined the New York Cosmos. He stopped playing in .... (5 *When?*) but he continued to work in the United States, where he helped to make football popular.

EXTRA TIME

Look at *World Club Magazine* on page 92.
Do activity 12.

Fluency

Writing: A Magazine Interview

A

Write a profile of a star you know, or invent one.

Stage 1: Preparation

Collect or invent information to answer these questions:

- When and where were you born?
- Tell us about your family and early life.
- What do you do in your free time?
- When did you get your first break?
- What important things did you do after that?
- What are you doing at the moment?

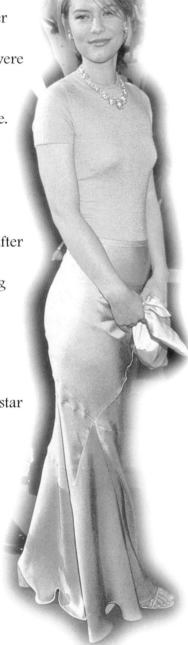

Stage 2: Writing

Write a magazine interview with your star (the questions and answers). You can include a photo.

Stage 3: Checking

Check your writing for:

- spelling and punctuation
- verb tenses
- linking words (*and, but, because, after that, later*)

Speaking: A Role-play

B

In pairs, take turns to interview a star on TV.

Stage 1: Preparation

Imagine you are a star. Think of answers to the questions in exercise A.

Stage 2: Speaking

In pairs, interview your partner. Ask him/her the questions from exercise A. If you want, you can act out the interview in front of the class.

Listening: A Song

C

Listen and answer the questions.

1 How long did the boy wait?
2 Who did the boy call?
3 What did the boy and Mary-Lou do?

Consolidation

Grammar

A

Copy and complete the text with the verbs in the correct form.

Leonardo DiCaprio always ¹ ... (want) to be an actor. But he ² ... (not study) acting, and he nearly ³ ... (not enter) the profession. As a teenager, his first agent ⁴ ... (not like) his name or his haircut! Leonardo ⁵ ... (decide) to try again and finally he ⁶ ... (play) some small parts on American TV. In 1993, he ⁷ ... (receive) his first big break in the film *This Boy's Life*. People soon ⁸ ... (call) him the new teenage rebel and he ⁹ ... (act) in films with superstars like Sharon Stone and Gene Hackman. After the film *Titanic,* he ¹⁰ ... (change) overnight into a superstar himself.

B

Write questions about Leonardo DiCaprio for these answers:

1 Yes, he always wanted to be an actor. (Did)
2 No, he didn't study acting. (Did)
3 In 1993, in *This Boy's Life*. (When)
4 They called him the new 'teenage rebel'. (What)
5 With people like Sharon Stone and Gene Hackman. (Who)

Vocabulary

C KEYWORDS

Complete the sentences with the words.

actor actress album brilliant charts concert
good-looking match player stadium terrible

1 Brad Pitt is my favourite ... . I think he's really ... too!
2 Ronaldo is a great football ... . He was ... in the ... yesterday.
3 The main ... wasn't very good. In fact, she was ... !
4 Their new ... is at the top of the ... . I've got a ticket for their ... next week – it's in the football ... .

Pronunciation: Consonant Sounds

D

Listen and repeat these words – be careful with the 'b' and 'v' sounds.

album / born / brilliant / favourite / interview / rebel / receive / television / terrible / very / victory / video

Module check

Grammar Reference

7 Past simple of regular verbs: affirmative and negative

	Affirmative	Negative
I You He She It We They	play**ed**	**didn't play**

- The **past simple** describes *an action that happened in the past*.

- In the past simple, *regular verbs* end in **d** or **ed**:
She arriv**ed** late.
Kate start**ed** at an acting school.

- We use the auxiliary **didn't** to form the *negative*:

- Remember! When we use **didn't**, *we don't add **d** or **ed** to the main verb*:
She **didn't arrive** at six o'clock.
Kate **didn't like** acting school.

8 Past simple of regular verbs: interrogative

Questions		
Did	I/you/ he/she/it/ we/they	**play?**

- We use the auxiliary **did** to form the *interrogative*.

- **Remember!** When we use **did**, *we don't add **d** or **ed** to the main verb*:
Did Kate **act** in Peter Pan?   Yes, she **did**.
Did her parents **like** it?   Yes, they **did**.
Did Kate **like** acting school?   No, she **didn't**.

Keyword Check

Films: actor, actress, break, character, part

Music: album, charts, classical music, concert, group, lyrics, musician, singer, song, stage

Sport: cycling, golf, gymnastics, match, net, player, racket, rally driving, stadium, tennis, tournament, victory

Verbs: act, arrive, be born, celebrate, change, earn, enjoy, play (a part in a film / a sport / a musical instrument), receive, start

Opinions: I think he's brilliant / good-looking / OK / terrible

Look through the module and add other important words to these lists.

1 **Look at Grammar References 7 and 8 on this page and complete Grammar File 4 in the Activity Book. Then do the *Test Yourself: Grammar* on page 32 of the Activity Book.**

2 **Look at the Keyword Check. Write important new words in your vocabulary book. Then do the *Test Yourself: Vocabulary* on page 32 of the Activity Book.**

Stars

46

SPIES
Lead-in

MODULE OBJECTIVES

IN THIS MODULE YOU WILL ...

Read	a picture story.
Listen	to directions and a story.
Talk	about spies and secret missions.
Practise	an ending to a story.
Write	past simple irregular verbs.

a 🔑 KEYWORDS

Match the words with the numbers on the mission sheet.

Example: 1 secret agent

b 🗨

Listen and check your answers.

---

mission   gadgets   secret agent   enemies
head of secret service

The World is Not Enough

1 007 — James Bond (British)

2 'M' (Bond's boss)

3 Renard and Electra - plan to control the world's oil supplies

4 to stop Renard starting nuclear war

5 Bond's BMW and ski jacket

5

13 Mission Anaconda

Agent: . . . .

Enemy agents: . . . .

. . . .

Mission: . . . .

Gadgets: . . . .

. . . .

A

Read the story. Copy and complete the mission sheet.

The British agent Paul McCann came back from his last mission in Tibet and met his boss Q in her office. She gave him his next mission: to find some secret plans for a military base on the moon before the Anacondan government got them!

Q told McCann about the mission. Dr Angela Unwin, a scientist from the island of Garuda, made the plans for a base on the moon. Then she talked to a British friend, Dr Bill Fell, about the plans. He was in contact with the top Anacondan agent in London, Samantha Kruger.

Q had a special briefcase. She gave it to McCann and put some special gadgets in it: a gun like a pen, a laser ring and a watch that was really a radio and computer. McCann's first job was to go to the Anacondan Embassy to spy on a meeting between Dr Fell and Samantha Kruger.

McCann left the office and went to the embassy. He saw Kruger and Fell inside and listened to their meeting about the secret plans. After the meeting, Kruger sent a secret message to her government in Anaconda, but McCann intercepted it with his radio.

B

Read the story again and answer these questions.

1 Which governments wanted to find the secret plans?

2 Which scientist made the plans for a base on the moon?

3 Where was she from?

4 Who did she talk to about the secret plans?

5 Why did McCann go to the Anacondan embassy?

6 How did McCann find out the message?

Language Focus: Past Simple Irregular Verbs (1)

C

When is the irregular verb form used?

AFFIRMATIVE	McCann **met** Q in her office.
NEGATIVE	He did not **meet** Dr Fell?
QUESTIONS	Did he **meet** Q?

Find the irregular forms of these verbs in the text.

Example: came back

come back / meet / give / get / tell / make / have / put / leave / go / see / send

See Grammar Reference 9 on page 56.

D

Put the verbs in the correct form.

Example: 1 had

TOP SECRET
ANACONDAN GOVERNMENT

To: Head of secret service
From: Agent Samantha Kruger

Tonight we ¹ ... (have) a meeting at the embassy. Dr Fell ² ... (come) and he ³ ... (tell) me about the secret plans. Last week he ⁴ ... (meet) Dr Unwin in London, but she ⁵ ... (not give) him the plans. She ⁶ ... (ask) for $10 million and Fell ⁷ ... (not get) the plans. They ⁸ ... (make) plans to meet tomorrow in Garuda City — in the Casablanca Café. I ⁹ ... (leave) the embassy immediately and ¹⁰ ... (go) directly to Heathrow Airport. I am now on a British Airways flight to Garuda City.

E

Invent your own mission. Think of these things:

- secret agents
- enemy
- head of secret service
- mission

Then write a secret message for your agents. Put it into a number code.

A1 B2 C3 D4 E5 F6 G7 H8 I9 J10 K11
L12 M13 N14 O15 P16 Q17 R18 S19
T20 U21 V22 W23 X24 Y25 Z26

Example: 13 5 5 20 9 14 7 (meeting)
23 9 20 8 (with) 4 18 (Dr)
19 9 12 22 5 19 20 5 18 (Silvester).

F

Give your message to your partner to decode. Then tell him/her about your mission.

G

In pairs, ask and answer questions about Mission Anaconda.

Example: A: Who did Dr Unwin tell about the secret plans?
B: She told Samantha Kruger.
A: No, wrong! She told Dr Fell.

(EXTRA TIME)

Look at *World Club Magazine* **on page 93 and do activity 13.**

Spies

49

14 Garuda City

A [KEYWORDS]

Match these words with the diagrams.

A	B	C	D	E	F

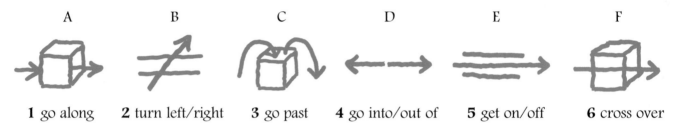

1 go along   **2** turn left/right   **3** go past   **4** go into/out of   **5** get on/off   **6** cross over

B

Listen and put the directions in order.

Example: b 1

a Go along this road – past the park, then turn right.

b When you get to the airport, get on the airport bus.

c Go past the cinema and on the left, in front of a supermarket, there is a café.

d Walk under a railway bridge and take the first turning on the left.

e Get off the bus at the Central Bus Station.

f Go out of the bus station and turn right.

Where on the map is the Casablanca Café – A, B, C or D?

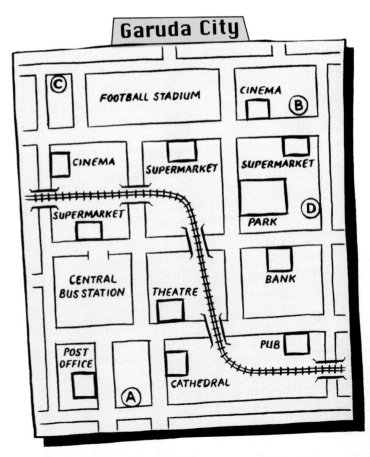

C

PRONUNCIATION: STRESSED WORDS
Listen to the directions again. Write down the stressed words.

Example: b get   airport   get   bus

Listen again and repeat the directions.

D

Complete these directions from the Central Bus Station to café A. Use the map to help you.

Get ¹ ... the bus at the Central Bus Station. Go ² ... of the station and turn right. Go ³ ... the street and go ⁴ ... the railway bridge. After the bridge take the second turning on the ⁵ ... Then turn ⁶ ... again and go ⁷ ... the pub. Go under another railway bridge and then turn ⁸ ... Go past the cathedral and turn right. The café is on your right.

Write directions for a shorter route.

E

In pairs, look at the map. Give your partner directions from the bus station to these places:

- the theatre
- the football stadium
- the bank
- the post office

F

Imagine you are McCann. Write a report about where Samantha Kruger went.

Examples: She got off the airport bus at the central bus station. Then she went out of the bus station...

G  DICTIONARY SKILLS

Look up the verbs in the mini-dictionary and complete the sentences with the correct preposition.

1 She gets .... at 7 o'clock every morning.
2 Please look .... my plants while I am on holiday.
3 I can't telephone you. They've cut my phone .... .
4 It's time to go to bed. Switch .... the television.
5 I looked ... my pen under the chair, but it wasn't there.

EXTRA TIME

Look at *World Club Magazine* on page 93 and do activity 14.

Spies

15 Escape!

A

Read the story and match the paragraphs with the pictures.

Example: 1 d

1 McCann went into the Casablanca café. He saw Dr Unwin and sat next to her — the Anacondan agents didn't know her. Dr Unwin thought McCann was an Anacondan agent and she put her briefcase on the floor next to him. McCann took the case and calmly walked out of the café.

2 After he left the café, McCann quickly read the secret plans and scanned them with his watch. Then he put the microchip in his ear and burnt the papers. Suddenly, he heard the Anacondan agents. He ran, but the agents caught him. They took him to a house and interrogated him, but he said nothing.

3 After the interrogation they put McCann in a room with a very small window with bars. He took his laser ring. Cut the bars of the window and escaped.

4 McCann ran from the house. In the street he saw a car and used his ring to get into it. Then he drove towards the airport. He was nearly there, when he saw two cars behind him with Anacondan agents in them. They started to shoot at him, and he drove faster...

Spies

B

Read the story again. True or false?

1 McCann knew who Dr Unwin was, but the Anacondans didn't.

2 McCann read the secret plans and memorised them.

3 He told the Anacondans about the plans.

4 He used his pen to escape from the room.

5 He got a taxi to go to the airport.

6 The Anacondans discovered his escape.

C

Complete these sentences.

Finally / Suddenly / Then / After

1 ... he read the plans, he scanned them.

2 ... he burnt them.

3 ... he heard the agents.

4 ... they caught him!

Language Focus: Simple Past Irregular Verbs (2)

D

Find the irregular forms of these verbs in the text.

> sit / think / take / read / burn / hear / run / catch / say / cut / drive

See Grammar Reference 9 on page 56.

E

Put the verbs in the simple past tense.

McCann[1] ... (drive) faster and faster but his car [2] ... (go) out of control. The car [3] ... (leave) the road and [4] ... (crash) into a tree. McCann [5] ... (get) out of the car quickly and [6] ... (run) into the forest. The Anacondan agents [7] ... (see) him and started to follow him. McCann [8] ... (hear) the agents and their dogs behind him.

F

PRONUNCIATION: IRREGULAR VERBS
Listen to the irregular verbs and repeat them.

Example: 1 drive   drove

G

Write down new irregular verbs from lessons 13 and 15 in your vocabulary book. In pairs, use your books to test your partner.

Example: A: Sit.

   B: Sitted.

   A: No, sat!

(EXTRA TIME)

Look at *World Club Magazine* on page 94 and do activity 15.

Fluency

Writing: A Story

A

Write the ending of the Mission Anaconda story.

Stage 1: Preparation

Look at the pictures. Imagine what happened between each picture. Use the words below to help you write notes.

> get into plane / start the engine / fly (flew) plane take off / agents shoot (shot) at him

Example: McCann – got into plane

Stage 2: Writing

Use your notes to write your ending. Use the words *after / then / suddenly / finally*. Then check for mistakes.

Stage 3: Feedback

In pairs, give your ending to your partner. Assess your partner's story like this:

> **5** brilliant – very exciting
>
> **3** good – interesting
>
> **1** poor – not very interesting

Speaking: Storytelling

B

Tell your ending to other students.

Stage 1: Preparation

Use your notes, not the written story, to practise telling the story.

Stage 2: Speaking

In groups of four, tell your story. Use gestures and sounds to help you (e.g. the sound of a gun). Don't worry if you make mistakes.

Listening: The End

C

Listen to another ending to the story. Answer these questions.

1 What did McCann have to cross?
   a a big road **b** a park **c** a river

2 Why did he have problems starting the plane?
   a because of the engine **b** because of the Anacondan agents **c** because he was not a pilot

3 Where did he fly after leaving Garuda?
   a Florida **b** Bermuda **c** Jamaica

4 What did Q tell McCann to do? **a** go on a new mission **b** go home **c** go on holiday

54

Consolidation

Grammar

A

Put the verbs in the past simple tense.

Yesterday, I [1] ... (not sleep) very well and [2] ... (have) a strange dream. In the morning, I [3] ... (have) breakfast and [4] ... (leave) home. Suddenly, on the bus to school I [5] ... (see) the woman from my dream behind me. When I [6] ... (get) off the bus she [7] ... (follow) me. I [8] ... (go) towards the school, but I [9] ... (hear) the woman behind me. I [10] ... (be) afraid and [11] ... (run) along the road to school. Then before lunch I [12] ... (see) her again. I [13] ... (ask) her, 'Why are you following me?' She [14] ... (answer) 'I'm the new head teacher!'

B

VERB GOLF

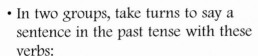

- In two groups, take turns to say a sentence in the past tense with these verbs:

  give / take / sit / read / burn / get / think / cut / put / hear / send / catch

- Every sentence is one 'shot'. If it is incorrect, take a second 'shot'. After six verbs each, the group with the fewest 'shots' is the winner (as in golf!).

Example: Group A:

Shot 1: Yesterday, I gav a present. (wrong)

Shot 2: Yesterday, I gave sweets. (no meaning)

Shot 3: Yesterday, I gave some sweets to my brother. (correct) Result: Group A used three 'shots'.

Vocabulary

C

Complete the sentences.

opposite / along / right / under / past / out / on / off / next / into

1 She got ... the bus and went to the centre of town. She got ... outside the cathedral.
2 Go ... of this building and turn ...
3 Go ... the railway bridge and go ... a cinema and a supermarket.
4 McCann walked ... the café and sat ... to Dr Ackerman.
5 Walk ... the street for 100 metres and the café is ... the railway station.

D

Match the two parts of the sentences.

1 Last night someone stole	**a** my best clothes.
2 Last Monday Q caught	**b** the radio from our car.
3 For the party I put on	**c** a meeting with the secret agent.
4 The secret service sent me	**d** a plane.
5 Yesterday, he had	**e** a message.

Pronunciation: Difficult Words

E

Can you say these words?

special / scientist / intercepted / bridge / message / gadgets / government / exchange

Now listen and repeat the words. Find three more difficult words in this module.

Module check

Grammar Reference

9 Past simple of irregular verbs: affirmative, negative and interrogative

- Verbs that *do not end in -ed in the past* are **irregular**.

- For example: know / knew
  - sit / sat
  - catch / caught

- *Affirmative:* use the **irregular** form:
McCann flew back to London.

- *Negative:* use **didn't + the infinitive**:
He **didn't write** his mission report on the plane.

- *Interrogative:* use **did** + subject + **the infinitive**:
Did he **see** agent Kruger?

(Always check the **correct form** and **spelling** of the verbs on the back cover of your Students' Book!)

Keyword Check

Spy words: code, enemy, mission, operations room, secret agent, secret message, secret plans, secret service, villain

Gadgets: umbrella gun, laser ring, newspaper bomb, watch radio and computer

Directions: cross over (a street), get on (a bus/train), get off (a bus/train), go along (the street), go into/out of (a building), go past (a place), go straight on, go under (a bridge), turn left/right, take the first turning on the left/right

Places: airport, bus station, cathedral, football stadium, post office, theatre, bank

Verbs: ask/asked, burn/burnt, catch/caught, come/came, cut/cut, drive/drove, find/found, get/got, give/gave, go/went, have/had, hear/heard, leave/left, make/made, meet/met, put/put, read/read, run/ran, say/said, see/saw, send/sent, take/took, tell/told, think/thought

Look through the module and add other important words to these lists.

1 **Look at Grammar Reference 9 on this page and complete Grammar File 5 in the Activity Book. Then do the *Test Yourself: Grammar* on page 39 of the Activity Book.**

2 **Look at the Keyword Check. Write important new words in your vocabulary book. Then do the *Test Yourself: Vocabulary* on page 39 of the Activity Book.**

FOOD

Lead-in

MODULE OBJECTIVES

IN THIS MODULE YOU WILL ...

Read — an advertisement, a history text and a menu.

Listen — to teenagers, a sports teacher and a poem.

Talk — about food and drink and going out.

Write — a fast-food menu.

Practise — using countable and uncountable nouns, making suggestions and expressing obligation.

---

a  KEYWORDS

Classify the food and drink in the photo.

> meat fruit fish drink vegetable
> dessert

b

In pairs, find out your partner's favourite fruit, drink, meat, vegetable and dessert.

Example: A: What's your favourite fruit?
  B: I love oranges. And you?

16 Banquets

A  KEYWORDS

Find these things in the picture.

> apples beans bread
> carrots eggs fish meat
> wine

B

Read the text and list things they didn't eat at medieval banquets.

Example: tomatoes

Medieval Life: Banquets

Rich people had banquets in their castle, but they didn't have a great variety of food. If you look at the picture, you can see there is some fish, a lot of meat, and there are a lot of beans! But there are only a few vegetables — and there aren't any potatoes or tomatoes, of course, because these things came to Europe from America.

Food wasn't very tasty in medieval times. As you can see, there is a little salt on the table, but there isn't any pepper, ketchup or mustard! And desserts? Well, there are some apples, but no tropical fruit like bananas. And remember, they didn't have fridges, so there isn't any ice-cream or chocolate mousse!

Language Focus 1: Countable and Uncountable Nouns

C

Look at the sentences in the boxes. How do you say the sentences in your language?

COUNTABLE	UNCOUNTABLE
Affirmative	**Affirmative**
There *are some* apples.	There *is some* fish.
Negative	**Negative**
There *aren't any* potatoes.	There *isn't any* ice-cream.
Questions	**Questions**
Are there *any* apples?	*Is* there *any* fish?
Short Answers	**Short Answers**
Yes, there *are.* / No, there *aren't*.	Yes, there *is.* / No, there *isn't*.

See Grammar Reference 10 on page 66.

Food

D

Use the information in the picture and text to write about these food items.

> wine tomatoes eggs bread ketchup
> bananas mustard carrots

Example: There is some wine.

E

Work in pairs.

Student A: Look at page 109: Exercise 4.

Student B: Ask and answer questions to find six differences between your picture and your partner's picture.

Example: In my picture there are a lot of bananas. Are there any bananas in your picture?

Language Focus 2: Quantity

F

Copy and complete the table with these words:

a little / a lot of / a few

COUNTABLE		UNCOUNTABLE
Questions How many beans are there?		**Questions** How much meat is there?
Large quantity There are [1] ... beans.		**Large quantity** There is [3] ... meat.
Small quantity There are [2] ... vegetables.		**Small quantity** There is [4] ... salt.

See Grammar Reference 11 on page 66.

G

Survey. Ask other pupils these questions for a food and drink survey. Record the results.

1 How many hamburgers do you eat every week?

2 How much ice-cream do you eat every week?

3 How much coke do you drink every week?

> **a** a lot   **b** a little/a few
> **c** doesn't eat/drink any

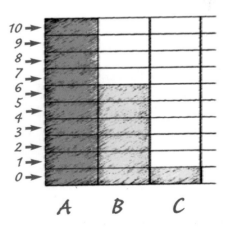

EXTRA TIME

Look at *World Club Magazine* on page 94. Do activity 16.

A

Look at the menu. How much do these orders cost?

1 A Mega Prince, big French fries and a big coke.

2 A Prince Chicken, a tuna salad and a big lemon drink.

3 A ham salad, a vanilla ice-cream and a small bottle of water.

Burger Prince

Big Prince
Quarter-pound burger with onion, ketchup and mustard. £1.20. With cheese £1.45.

Mega Prince
Double burger with tomato, lettuce, onion, mustard and ketchup. £2.30. With cheese £2.55.

Desserts
Ice cream sundae (chocolate, vanilla or strawberry). 80p Apple pie. 85p

Drinks
Big coke, orange or lemon. 85p
Mega coke, orange or lemon. £1.15
Mineral water (33 ml bottle). 55p

Prince Chicken
Chicken burger, lettuce and mayonnaise. £1.15.

Salad
Ham or tuna with tomato, cucumber, carrot, onion. Choice of three dressings – vinaigrette, mayonnaise or barbecue. 85p.

French Fries
Regular 50p, Big 85p, Mega £1.10.

B

What do you think these people choose?

Larry He is very hungry and thirsty. He also likes sweet things.

Marie She doesn't eat much meat. She likes health foods.

Listen and check your predictions. How much do they each spend?

C

Listen to Larry and Marie and complete the dialogue with these *let's*, *don't* and *do*.

Larry: You don't like burgers, then.

Marie: No, not really.

Larry: [1] ... you want to go for an ice cream?

Marie: You've got one!

Larry: I can eat another!

Marie: No, [2] ... go for a walk.

Larry: I know. Why [3] ... we go to the cinema?

Marie: Yes, good idea.

D

In pairs, imagine you are deciding where to go on Friday, Saturday and Sunday. Make suggestions and agree on different places.

for a pizza	for a drink	for a walk
to the cinema	to the park	to the sports

Example: A: Let's go for a pizza on Saturday night.

B: I don't know. Why don't we go to the cinema? I want to see the new Spielberg film.

Tell the class where you agreed to go.

E LONGMAN DICTIONARY SKILLS

Singular or plural? Countable or uncountable? Use the mini-dictionary and complete the sentences.

1 Let's have chips this evening. Have we got any ... ?   (potato)

2 My favourite dish is ... and cream. (strawberry)

3 Please go and buy some ... and some ... . (fruit / tomato)

4 The salad was a few lettuce ... under some ... leaf / mayonnaise)

5 He ordered two ... with a little ... .   (coffee / milk)

EXTRA TIME

Look at *World Club Magazine* on page 95.
Do activity 17.

Food

18 Healthy Living

A KEYWORDS

Classify these things as healthy (H) or unhealthy (U).

> bread   chocolate   cigarettes   fried eggs
> fresh fruit   fresh vegetables   meat   milk
> pasta   potatoes   sweets

B

Listen to the sports teacher and check your answers to exercise A.

C

Listen again. Which foods give us:

1 carbohydrates?

2 vitamins?

3 proteins?

Language Focus: Obligation

D

Listen and complete these sentences with these words:

have to / don't have to / must / mustn't

1 You ... eat lots of fresh fruit and vegetables.
2 You ... eat things like bread, potatoes and pasta.
3 You ... eat things like chocolate and sweets.
4 You ... go on a special diet.

What does each sentence express?

obligation / no obligation / prohibition

E

Read about the boy's routine and then complete the doctor's orders.

On Saturdays, for breakfast, I always have fried bread, sausages and eggs. Then I watch the cartoons on TV all morning. For lunch I usually go into town and have a pizza – double cheese with mushrooms and a big glass of coke. In the afternoon I play games on my play station. In the evening I usually stay in and watch some videos. On Sundays I go jogging for about three hours!

1 You ... eat a fried breakfast.
2 You ... eat a better lunch.
3 You ... to do more exercise.
4 You ... watch less television.
5 You ... to go jogging for hours.
6 You ... to do a little exercise each day.

F

Complete these sports tips with before, while or after.

Example: 1 Before

1 ... you play any sport, you must do some warm-up exercises.
2 Don't eat ... you are playing!
3 If possible, drink something. For example, cyclists drink water ... they are racing.
4 Do some exercises ... you finish – this is called 'warming down'!
5 Remember, you mustn't eat a lot ... you swim.

Food

(EXTRA TIME)

Look at *World Club Magazine* on page 96. Do activity 18.

Fluency

Writing: A Menu

A

Write a menu for a fast-food bar.

Stage 1: Preparation

Invent a name for your restaurant.
Write a list of the food it sells.

Example:

burgers   sausages   steaks   salads   desserts   drinks

Stage 2: Writing

Write the menu with ingredients and prices.
Look again at the menu in Lesson 17.

Stage 3: Checking

Check your menu for spelling.

Stage 4: Feedback

In groups, show each other your menus. Then give your opinions.

Example: I think these sausages are absolutely delicious / tasty / horrible.

Speaking: A Role-play

B

In groups, act out a scene in your invented restaurant.

Stage 1: Preparation

Decide who is the waiter/waitress and who are the friends.
Use the menu from Lesson 17 or your own menu.

Stage 2: Speaking

Order your meal from the waiter/waitress.
While you are waiting, suggest where to go tonight.

Example: Why don't we go to see the new *Star Wars* film?

Listening: A Poem

C

Listen and complete this poem.

I know a man from Ghana,
Who has for a pet a pirhana,
It eats chocolate ...,
And drinks fruit ...,
Its favourite by far is ...

His fish now lives in a lake,
Drinking afternoon ... with some ...,
One day for a joke,
He gave it some ...,
And the caffeine now keeps it awake!

 **Consolidation**

Grammar

A

Two people are checking what they have got in a shop. Complete this dialogue.

few / any (x3) / lot / little (x2) / many / is / some / are / much

A: Have we got [1] ... bananas?

B: Yes, but we've only got a [2] ...

A: How [3] ... kilos?

B: About one and a half.

A: And have we got [4] ... tea?

B: Oh yes. We've got a [5] ... of tea. There [6] ... about 300 packets!

A: OK. And what about me? How much milk [7] ... there?

B: There isn't [8] ...

A: And coffee? How [9] ... is there?

B: There's only a [10] ...

A: And cheese?

B: Again, there's only a [11] ...

A: So we need [12] ... cheese.

B

Complete these sentences with these words.

must / mustn't / have / don't have

1 You ... eat a lot of sweets – they're bad for your teeth.

2 You ... eat more fresh fruit.

3 You ... to do a lot of exercise every day – twice a week is OK.

4 You ... to drink a lot of water in hot weather.

5 You ... eat in class.

6 You ... to drink milk – it's good for teeth and bones.

Vocabulary

C   KEYWORDS

Copy and complete the vocabulary network with words from this module.

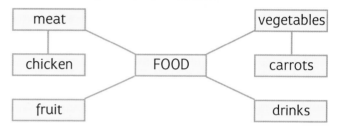

```
  meat                    vegetables
  chicken      FOOD        carrots
  fruit                     drinks
```

D KEYWORDS
MEMORY GAME

- In groups, play this memory game.

Example: A: On my list I've got a kilo of apples.

B: On my list I've got a kilo of apples and some cheese.

C: On my list I've got a kilo of apples, some cheese and a can of cola.

- If you make a mistake, you are out of the game.

Pronunciation: Plural Endings

E

Listen to the ending of these words.

Group 1: (/ z /)   potato**es**

Group 2: (/ s /)   carrot**s**

Group 3: (/ ɪz /)   sausag**es**

Now listen and repeat these words. Then classify them.

beans / drinks / oranges / burgers / bananas / sandwiches / cokes / eggs / steaks / sauces / sardines / apples

Module check

Grammar Reference

10 Countable and uncountable nouns

• We use **some** in *affirmative sentences*:

I'd like **some** milk and **some** biscuits, please.

• We use **any** in *negative sentences*:

I'm sorry! We haven't got **any** biscuits.
We haven't got **any** milk.

• We usually use **any** in *questions*.

Is there **any** milk in the bottle?
Are there **any** biscuits in the box?

11 Quantity

• **Countable** nouns:
• We express indefinite quantities with **a few/a lot**:

a few carrots   **a lot of** oranges

• We ask questions with **How many ... ?**
• We answer with **a few/a lot.**

How many carrots are there?   A few.
How many oranges are there?   A lot.

• **Remember!** In *complete answers or affirmative sentences*, we use **a lot of**:

I eat **a lot of** vegetables.

• **Uncountable** nouns:
• We express indefinite quantities with **a little/a lot**:

a little wine   **a lot of** cheese

• We ask questions with **How much ... ?**
• We answer with **a little/a lot.**

How much wine is there?   A little.
How much cheese is there?   A lot.

• **Remember!** In *complete answers or affirmative sentences*, we use **a lot of**:

I eat **a lot of** salad.

Keyword Check

General: breakfast, delicious, dessert, dinner, lunch, menu, tasty

Fruit: apple, banana, lemon, orange, strawberry, tomato

Vegetables: beans, carrot, cucumber, lettuce, onion, potato

Meat: burger, chicken, sausage, steak

Fish: sardines, tuna

Drinks: coffee, coke, milk, mineral water, orange juice, wine

Other food: bread, cheese, chocolate mousse, eggs, ice cream, ketchup, mayonnaise, mustard, pepper, pizza, salt, sandwich, sweets

Health: carbohydrates, proteins, vitamins

Suggestions: Let's ... , Why don't we ... , Do you want to ...

Can you add more words to these lists?

1 Look at Grammar References 10 and 11 on this page and complete Grammar File 6 in the Activity Book. Then do the *Test Yourself: Grammar* on page 46 of the Activity Book.

2 Look at the Keyword Check. Write important new words in your vocabulary book. Then do the *Test Yourself: Vocabulary* on page 46 of the Activity Book.

Food

TOMORROW'S WORLD

MODULE OBJECTIVES

IN THIS MODULE YOU WILL ...

Read — a magazine article and newspaper reports.

Listen — to a radio programme.

Talk — about the future.

Write — a report about the future.

Practise — the future with *will* and the present perfect.

Lead-in

a KEYWORDS

In pairs, decide which things in the box:

- exist now
- are possible in the near future
- are impossible

intelligent computers   hotels on the Moon
contact with aliens   large spaceships   video phones
interplanetary travel domestic robots   time travel

Use the mini-dictionary to help you.

b

Tell the class.

Example: Intelligent computers do not exist now, but we think they're possible in the near future.

19 The Year 2050

A 🔑 KEYWORDS

Which of the words are similar in your language?

> laser machine card virtual reality
> electronic computer petrol

B

Read the article. List things we will or won't have in the year 2050.

Example: laser toilets (Yes); water toilets (No)

C

Read the text again. Which changes are good and which are bad? Tell the class.

Example: I think virtual reality holidays are bad.

How will we live in fifty years time? Here are some predictions.

- We will have new laser toilets in our homes. We won't have water toilets because water will be very expensive.

- Very few people will smoke and cigarettes will be illegal.

- We will use our eyes for personal identification – for example to get into our homes. We will not have I.D. cards.

- We won't have money – we will use portable cards.

- We will go on 'virtual reality' holidays – because they will be cheaper than real ones.

- Most books will disappear – we will only have one electronic book. But we will change the content of our electronic book when we want.

- We will have portable computers in our shoes and communicate information to other people by touch.

- Petrol cars will disappear. We will have electric or solar cars and more people will use public transport.

Tomorrow's world

68

Language Focus: Future - *Will*

D

Copy and complete the tables with words from the text.

AFFIRMATIVE		
I / you / he / she / it / we / they	¹ ... ('ll)	have an electronic book.

NEGATIVE		
I / you / he / she / it / we / they	² ... (n't)	smoke cigarettes.

QUESTIONS			
How	³ ...	I / you / he / she / it / we / they	live?

See Grammar Reference 12 on page 76.

E

Use the words to write sentences about life in the future.

Example: 1 Women will have better jobs. More men will work in the home.

1 Women / have / better jobs. More men / work / in the home.
2 Most forests / disappear. Wood / become / very expensive.
3 Most children / not go / school. They study / home / the Internet
4 People / not work. Robots / do / work.
5 Scientists / find / a cure for cancer and AIDS.
6 People / not buy / books. They / use / the Internet.

Do you agree or disagree with the predictions?

F

Write five of your predictions. Use the ideas to help you.

> life – get better/worse
> clothes – become more/less exciting
> homes – become bigger/smaller
> people – become fatter/thinner
> football – become less/more popular

G

In pairs, discuss your predictions.

Example: A: I think life will get worse.

B: I don't agree. It will get better!

H LONGMAN DICTIONARY SKILLS

Circle the correct word. Use the mini-dictionary.

1 We arrived at the aircraft / airport at 6 o'clock for the 7 o'clock flight.
2 I always choose ice cream for my dessert / desert.
3 They live on the tenth floor of a ten-story / storey building.
4 The comedy was very amusing / amazing and we laughed a lot.
5 The Internet is very useful / useless to find information.

(EXTRA TIME)

Look at *World Club Magazine* on page 96. Do activity 19.

Tomorrow's world

20 Your Future

A 🔑 KEYWORDS

Write the personal qualities needed for each job.

Example: nurse – good with people/practical

jobs: nurse / artist / translator / carpenter / scientist / explorer / business person

qualities: adventurous / ambitious / creative / good at languages / good with people / intelligent / practical

Tomorrow's world

B

Listen to the fortune teller and complete the table.

	Mary	Ricardo
personal qualities		
jobs		

C

Listen again and answer the questions.

1 Where will Mary travel?
2 What will she win?
3 Where will she meet her boyfriend?
4 What languages will Ricardo learn?
5 Where will he work?
6 How many children will he have?

D

PRONUNCIATION: CONTRACTIONS

Listen to the sentences and count the words.

Example: 1 You'll travel to many places.   (6 words)

Listen again and repeat the sentences.

E

Match the two parts.

1 You won't have a lot of money.
2 You will travel a lot
3 John will speak six languages
4 Sarah won't do well at school.
5 Tom will do well at school

a *but* you won't go to Australia.
b *but* he won't go to university.
c *However,* she will get a good job.
d *but* he won't use them in his job.
e *However,* you will be happy.

When do we use *but* and when do we use *however*?

F

PREDICTION GAME

- Write six *yes/no* questions about your future in the next five years.

  Example: Will I study Japanese?

- In pairs, find the answers to your partner's questions. Open a book (without looking!) and add the digits of the page number. If the final number is even, the answer is 'yes', if the number is odd, the answer is 'no'.

  Example: 17 = 1 + 7 = 8 – answer 'Yes'.

- In pairs, ask and answer questions about your 'fortune'.

  Example: A: Will I study Japanese?
  B: Yes, you will.

Look at *World Club Magazine* on page 96. Do activity 20.

Tomorrow's World

21 Alien Invasion

a

"They are from the planet Kropton"

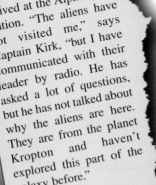

The alien ship has now arrived at the Alpha space station. "The aliens have not visited me," says Captain Kirk, "but I have communicated with their leader by radio. He has asked a lot of questions, but he has not talked about why the aliens are here. They are from the planet Kropton and haven't explored this part of the galaxy before."

b

"I believe the aliens have not planned to invade us. I think Admiral Ballard made a tragic mistake. We have decided to let the Kroptonians on Earth for their spaceships. The Kroptonians have decided to give the Earth advanced space and medical technology. This is the beginning of..."

c

Alien missiles have destroyed several military bases in the United States. This happened after a nuclear attack on the spaceship ordered by US Admiral Ballard. Chairwoman Mobastik has decided to go to Station Alpha to negotiate with the alien chief...

d

Scientists have received radio signals from space. They have decoded a message – some aliens have asked permission to stop at Earth to repair a spaceship. The Chairwoman of the U.N., Celia Mobastik, has transmitted a message with an invitation to visit Earth.

A 🔑 KEYWORDS

Find these things in the pictures.

> military base   spaceship   observatory
> space station   alien   radio signal
> nuclear missile

B 📖

Read the newspaper extracts and put them in the right order.

Example: 1 d

C 📖

Read the reports again and answer the questions.

1 Why did the aliens want to come to Earth?
2 Why did the aliens destroy the US military bases?
3 Why did Ms Mobastik go to Station Alpha?
4 What was the agreement between Mobastic and the Kroptonians?

Language Focus: Present Perfect

D

Copy and complete the tables with *have* or *has*.

AFFIRMATIVE				
I / you / we / they	¹ ... ('ve)	received	a message from space.
he / she / it	² ... ('s)	asked	a lot of questions.
NEGATIVE				
I / you / we / they	³ ... (haven't)	planned	to invade the Earth.
he / she / it	⁴ ... (hasn't)	talked	about why they are here.
QUESTIONS				
Have	I / you / we / they	talked	to the aliens?
⁵ ...	he / she / it	arrived?	

See Grammar Reference 13 on page 76.

E

Put the verbs into the present perfect tense.

Example: 1 We have arrived at Earth, but we...

1 We (arrive) at Earth, but we (not start) to repair the ship.

2 I (talk) to humans and I (look) around their space station. It is very primitive!

3 I (not decide) what to do. I (talk) about the situation with my assistant.

4 We (examine) the Earth with our telescopes. The humans (not look) after it well.

5 Two military spaceships (arrive) to look at us but they (not make) contact.

6 I (finish) my report for the Kroptonian government – but I (not transmit) it.

F

Look at the list of the things. Write sentences about the things you have done today.

Example: I have not watched TV.
I have phoned a friend.

watch TV / phone a friend / listen to the radio / use a computer / finish homework / clean room / visit a friend / organise your file / play tennis / study English / talk to your grandmother / plan the weekend

G

Work in pairs.

Student A: Look at page 109: Exercise 5.

Student B: Find out about your partner's qualities. Ask what he or she has done today/this week/this month. Then give your opinions. After that, answer your partner's questions.

Example: Have you helped anybody this week? What did you do? ...
I think you are good with people but you aren't ambitious. You will be a good nurse.

> EXTRA TIME

Look at *World Club Magazine* on page 97. Do activity 21.

Tomorrow's world

Fluency

Writing: News

A

Imagine you are in the year 2050. In pairs or groups write a TV news programme.

Stage 1: Planning

Think of news items from these areas:
- politics: visits of presidents, etc.
- scientific discoveries: inventions, cures, etc.
- entertainment: films, music, sport, etc.

Include the ages of the people (in fifty years time!).

Example: Tony Blair, 97, Earth Ambassador, has visited the President of the Moon.

Stage 2: Writing

Write your news broadcast.
Use the expressions in the box to help you:

> Good evening. This is the nine o'clock news. Here are the headlines.
>
> There is some important (scientific / film / sports / music) news. Here is some more news from...

Stage 3: Checking

Check your news for simple mistakes.

Speaking: Presenting the News

B

In groups, broadcast your news.

Stage 1: Preparation

Divide up the news sections:

Example: Tina – politics/sport, Alberto – science/film, Javier – music

Practise giving the news.

Stage 2: Speaking

Present the news to the rest of the class.

Listening: The News 2050

C 🖭

Listen to the TV news. Answer the questions.

1 What planet has the President of the United Nations visited? a) Mars b) Jupiter c) Neptune
2 How many tourists have disappeared on the Moon? a) ten b) five c) three
3 What have scientists discovered? a) dinosaur fossils on the Moon b) life on the Sun c) an alien base in the Antarctic
4 What planet has won the Galactic Football Cup? a) the Earth b) Mars c) Venus
5 What film has received twenty Oscars? a) Alien 76 b) Star Wars 34 c) Space Titanic
6 Who has Leonardo DiCaprio married? a) Kate Winslet b) Martina Hingis c) Claudia Schiffer
7 How many records have *The Space Girls* now made? a) 102 b) 32 c) 132
8 Where have the Rolling Stones played a concert? a) London b) Albacete c) New York

Consolidation

Grammar

A

Put the words into the correct order.

1 be / in 2020 / I / at / won't / school
2 live / will / on other planets / people /in the future / ?
3 she / that / finished / science homework / has / ?
4 today / talked / I / to her / haven't
5 will / longer / in the year 2050 / people / live
6 a scientist / a new / invented / microscope

B

Complete the sentences with your predictions.

1 Manchester United (will/will not) win the European Cup next year.
2 People (will/will not) have longer holidays in the future.
3 Pollution (will/will not) be worse in the year 2010.
4 Spain (will/will not) win the next World Cup.
5 People (will/will not) live on the Moon in the next ten years.
6 Scientists (will/will not) discover life on Jupiter.
7 People (will/will not) drive flying cars.
8 We (will/will not) have portable computers in our shoes.
9 Space travel (will/will not) be a common practice.
10 People (will/will not) be healthier.

Vocabulary

C  KEYWORDS

Match the words.

1	computer	**a**	reality
2	virtual	**b**	base
3	portable	**c**	signal
4	time	**d**	science
5	radio	**e**	travel
6	military	**f**	computer

D

Copy and complete the table with adjectives from this module.

noun	adjective
intelligence	intelligent
expense	
person	
ambition	
adventure	
practice	
creativity	

Pronunciation: 'o' Sounds

E

Listen to these words.

Group 1: /ɒ/   h<u>o</u>t
Group 2: /eʊ/   h<u>o</u>tel

Classify these words. Then listen and check your answer.

contact / not / smoke / tropical / home / job / don't / lot / though / won't / radio / option

Module check

Grammar Reference

12 Future simple (with *will*): affirmative, negative and interrogative

Affirmative		Negative			Questions		
I You He She It We They	will think	I You He She It We They	will not (won't)	think	Will	I you he she it we they	think?

- We use **will** to talk about the future.

- *Affirmative:* **will** + infinitive:

People **will speak** more English.

He**'ll become** a famous doctor.

- *Negative:* **will not** + infinitive:

People **will not** smoke.   I **won't forget** you.

- *Interrogative:* **will** + subject + infinitive:

Will life **get** better?   Where **will** all these people **live**?

13 Present perfect: affirmative, negative and interrogative

	Affirmative	Negative	Questions		
I You We They	have seen ('ve seen)	have not seen (haven't seen)	Have	I you we they	seen?
He She It	has seen ('s seen)	has not seen (hasn't seen)	Has	he she it	seen?

- The **present perfect** describes *an action that happened but is still important now.*
- It is formed with *the auxiliary* **have** *and the past participle.*
- *Affirmative:* **has/have** + **past participle**

I **have finished** my report.   We**'ve cleaned** our room.

- *Negative:* **has/have** + not + **past participle**

They **have** not **organised** their files.

He **hasn't used** the computer.

- *Interrogative:* **has/have** + subject + **past participle**

Has she **made** that phone call?

Have you **finished** your homework?

Keyword Check KEYWORDS

Machines: portable computer, laser, robot, satellite, spaceship, space shuttle, video phone

General: cancer, government, the Internet, pensions, interplanetary travel, scientist, time travel

Jobs: artist, business person, carpenter, explorer, translator, scientist

Personality adjectives: adventurous, ambitious, creative, intelligent, practical

Other adjectives: cheap, electronic, expensive, illegal, primitive

Verbs: destroy, explore, invade, repair, look after (a person), look around (a place), look at (something)

Compound words: computer science, portable computer, public transport, virtual reality, radio signal

Look through the module and add other important words to these lists.

1 Look at Grammar References 12 and 13 on this page and complete Grammar File 7 of the Activity Book. Then do the *Test Yourself: Grammar* on page 53 of the Activity Book.

2 Look at the Keyword Check. Write important new words in your vocabulary book. Then do the *Test Yourself: Vocabulary* on page 53 of the Activity Book.

Tomorrow's world

MACHINES
Lead-in

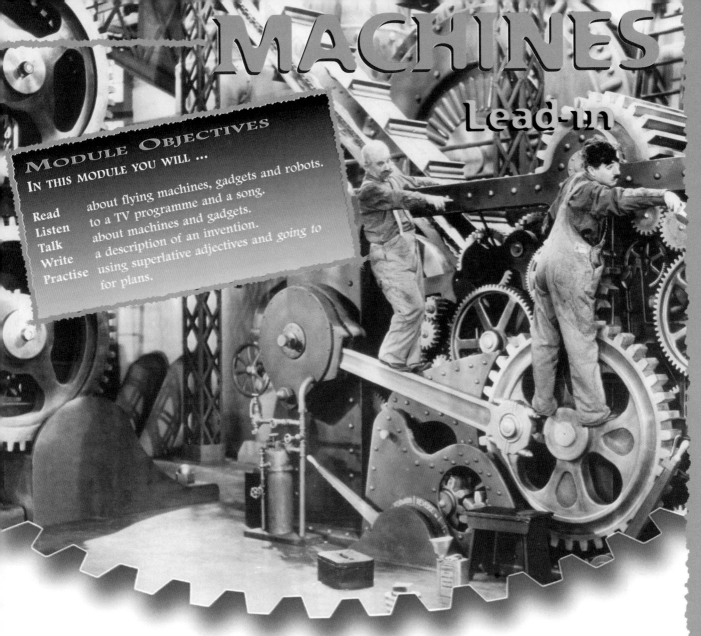

MODULE OBJECTIVES

IN THIS MODULE YOU WILL ...

Read   about flying machines, gadgets and robots.
Listen   to a TV programme and a song.
Talk   about machines and gadgets.
Write   a description of an invention.
Practise using superlative adjectives and going to
          for plans.

a KEYWORDS

Classify these machines. They may go in more than one column.

> car   computer   microwave oven
> motorbike   photocopier   rocket
> vacuum cleaner   video player

Transport	Home	School
car		

b

MACHINES GAME

- In pairs, write down more machines for each column. With another pair, take turns to say machines from your list. The pair with the longest list wins.

Example: A: Transport – aeroplane
B: School – pocket calculator

22 Flying Machines

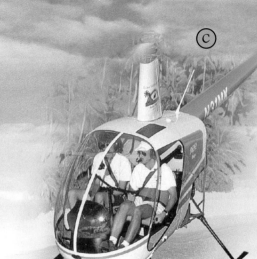

Flight Factfile

1 Oliver of Malmesbury probably made the earliest flight in 1010. He put wings on his arms and jumped from a church – he flew a short distance but broke both his legs!

2 Leonardo da Vinci (1452-1519) designed a helicopter!

3 The strangest passenger list was for the first hot-air balloon flight in 1783. A chicken, a duck and a sheep went up in the Montgolfier brothers' balloon!

4 Otto Lilienthal made several controlled flights between 1891 and 1896 – in a hang-glider!

5 Transatlantic airships were popular in the 1920s, but they were probably the most dangerous method of transport – they were full of hydrogen gas!

6 In 1998, Brian Milton made the shortest flight around the world in an open-top flying machine. He was in the air for 120 days – in a microlight!

7 The largest passenger aeroplane is the Boeing 747-400 – it can carry 567 people!

A 🔒 KEYWORDS

Match the pictures with these words and texts.

> aeroplane   airship   hang-glider   helicopter
> hot-air balloon   microlight   human flight

Example: picture A: airship – text 5

B 📖

Read the text. Are these statements true or false?

1 Leonardo da Vinci made the first flight in a helicopter.

2 Some animals made the first flight in a hot-air balloon.

3 Otto Lilienthal made the first powered flight.

4 Airships flew across the Atlantic in the 1920s.

5 The largest aeroplane can carry 747 people.

Machines

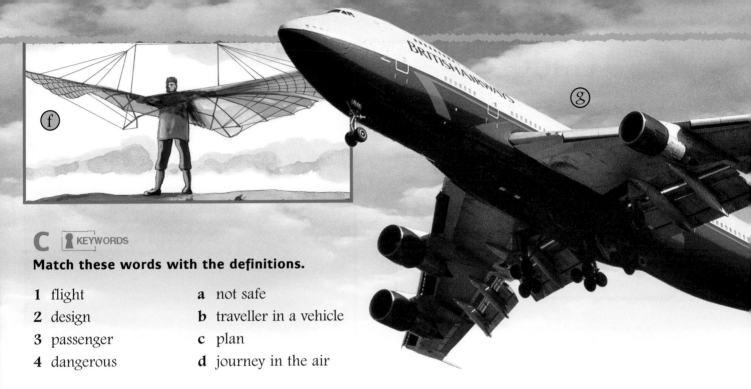

C KEYWORDS

Match these words with the definitions.

1 flight
2 design
3 passenger
4 dangerous

a not safe
b traveller in a vehicle
c plan
d journey in the air

Language Focus: Superlatives

D

Copy and complete the table with words from the text.

Adjective	Superlative
strange	the strangest
early	
dangerous	
good / bad	the best / the worst

E

Match these rules with the adjectives in the table.

1 two-syllable adjective ending in 'y' – use 'iest'
2 one-syllable adjective – use 'est'
3 irregular adjectives – irregular superlative
4 more than one syllable adjective – use 'most'

See Grammar Reference 14 on page 86.

F

Complete the sentences with superlative adjectives.

Example: 1 smallest

1 The... (small) plane is Bumble Bee Two – it is 2.64 m long and weighs 179.6 kg.
2 Horatio Phillips built the ... (silly) aeroplane in the 1890s – it had twenty wings!
3 The ... (famous) airship is the Hindenburg – it crashed in 1937.
4 The Antonov An-225 Mriya is the ... (heavy) plane – it weighs 600 tonnes!
5 Helicopters are the ... (useful) aircraft for rescue operations.
6 The Hercules 'flying boat' has got the ... (long) wings – they measure 97.5 m.
7 One of the ... (unusual) planes is the American Stealth Bomber – it is made of plastic!

(EXTRA TIME)

Look at *World Club Magazine* on page 97.
Do activity 22.

A KEYWORDS

Look at the list of gadgets. Which is the most useful? Tell the class.

> automatic car-door opener
> pocket calculator · mobile phone
> smoke alarm   TV remote control

Example: I think the most useful gadget is the mobile phone. You can...

B

Match the names of these inventions with the pictures:

back scratcher's shirt / earring safety nets / personal rain saver

C

Listen to the interview and complete the texts.

CHINDOGU

THE JAPANESE ART OF USELESS INVENTIONS!

You need this invention [1] ... earrings can be expensive or they can have sentimental value. You attach a small net on each shoulder below your ears [2] ... you can catch an earring if it falls off!

Basically, this gadget is an umbrella, [3] ... it keeps you dry. It also collects water – put it upside down [4] ... the water can go down a tube into a plastic bag on your shoulder. This invention is practical [5] ... you can save hundreds of litres of precious water every year!

Have you ever asked a friend to scratch your back? This amazing T-shirt has a special map [6] ... you can locate your itch accurately. Now your friend can find the exact position immediately.

GET IT QUICK! IT'S ON G5

Machines

80

D

Complete these descriptions with:

because (x2) / so / to

THE PORTABLE ZEBRA CROSSING

You need this invention [1] ... it is dangerous to cross roads. Also, there isn't usually a zebra crossing when you want one.

[2] ... solve this problem, we have invented the Portable Zebra Crossing. It is a black and white plastic carpet. Roll it out across the road [3] ... you can cross when you want!

E

GUESS THE GADGET

- Write a sentence about a gadget in this lesson.
- Read your sentence to your group.
- The other students guess the gadget.

Example: You can collect water with this.

THE WALK 'N' WASH

Washing clothes takes time and it's boring too. Simply put these two plastic boxes on your legs when you are playing football or tennis. You can do the washing and have fun [4] ... each box holds three litres of water and clothes.

F

PRONUNCIATION: CONTRACTIONS

Listen and write down each sentence. Is the contraction *it has* or *it is*?

Example: 1 Basically, it's an umbrella. (it is)

> ### Did you know?
>
> Japanese 'chindogu' gadgets really exist – but you can't buy them.

(EXTRA TIME)

Look at *World Club Magazine* on page 97. Do activity 23.

Machines

A WORLD OF ROBOTS

Imagine robots running, jumping, throwing and swimming. A scene from science fiction? Not really. Scientists have had small international competitions with robots since 1990, and they are going to get bigger.

1 Today robots work with radioactive materials and at the bottom of the sea. Scientists have developed new robots – they are going to help with fire-fighting and rescue operations.

2 Computers control 'driverless' trains in many modern cities; soon you are going to see robot buses in your city centre.

3 This is going to be a big area for robots. Obviously, you aren't going to visit a robot doctor in a white coat!

But scientists have designed artificial intelligence machines that can make a diagnosis and then make suggestions to a human doctor.

4 Robots have done some of our boring or dirty jobs for many years. Scientists have designed many new machines and in the next few years, there are going to be more factories with robot workers.

5 The first intelligent life to explore our solar system isn't going to be human. Robots have explored Mars, and scientists are going to use them for other planets.

A  KEYWORDS

What things do you think robots will do in the future?

> play sport   fight fires   drive buses
> diagnose illnesses   explore planets

Read the text and check your predictions.

B

Match the headings with the numbered paragraphs.

Transport / Dangerous Jobs / Medicine / Space Exploration / Factories

Example: 1 Dangerous Jobs

C  KEYWORDS

Find the opposite of these words in the text.

> safe small old natural interesting clean

Language Focus: Plans with *Going to*

D

Copy and complete the tables.

AFFIRMATIVE

He / She / It	am	going to	see robot buses.
You / We / They	¹ ...		
	² ...		

NEGATIVE

He / She / It	am not	⁵ ... to	visit a robot doctor.
You / We / They	³ ...		
	⁴ ...		

QUESTIONS

What	am	I	going to	do there?
How	⁶ ...	he / she / it		help us?
When	⁷ ...	you / we / they		live in a robot world?

See Grammar Reference 15 on page 86.

E

Put the words in the correct order to make sentences.

Example: 1 NASA are going to send astronauts to Mars.

1 send / are / NASA / going to / to Mars / astronauts

2 is / how long / the journey / take? / going to

3 it / going to / take / about seven months / is

4 build / going to / they / aren't / a space station there

5 the astronauts / are / stay / going to / a long time?

6 going to / am / follow / on the Internet / I / the mission

F

Work in pairs.

Student A: Look at page 109: Exercise 6.

Student B: Ask your partner about pictures 1, 3, 5 and 7 and answer questions about pictures 2, 4 and 6.

Example: Number 1. Is the boy going to play basketball or badminton?

G LONGMAN DICTIONARY SKILLS

Find compound nouns in the mini-dictionary and ask questions like these:

What is the word for:

• a machine which *plays CDs*?

• an insect that *hops* in the *grass*?

• a *person* who works in *business*?

(EXTRA TIME)

**Look at *World Club Magazine* on page 97.
Do activity 24.**

Machines

83

Fluency

Writing: A Description

A

**Write a description of
a real gadget or invent your own.**

Stage 1: Preparation

Do a quick drawing or plan of the gadget.
Use a bilingual dictionary to find useful words.
Here are some ideas:

> *Real gadgets:* smoke alarm, pocket translator,
> virtual pet, key-ring light
>
> *Silly gadgets:* a gadget to bring you drinks in
> the swimming pool, a pair of trainers to
> help you jump, a gadget to hold a book
> when you are reading in the shower

Stage 2: Writing

Write sentences about the following:
- the reason for the invention
- what it looks like
- how it works

Include a neat drawing or diagram in your
description.

Stage 3: Checking

Check your writing for punctuation and
spelling. Have you included linking words from
Lesson 23D (*basically, because, to, so*)?

Speaking: Telling Others

B

Describe your gadget to your group.

Stage 1: Preparation

Look at your description of a gadget and write a
list of important words.

Stage 2: Speaking

Describe your gadget to your group. Do not read
your written description – use your list of
important words.

Stage 3: Feedback

In groups, look at the drawings and descriptions.
Decide which is the silliest or the most useful.
Tell the class.

Listening: A Song

C

Listen to the song and answer the questions.

1 What gadget is the song about?
2 What is the operator doing?
3 What happens when you press a 'special key'?

 # Consolidation

Grammar

A

Complete the sentences with superlative adjectives.

1 The ... (fast) computers can perform over 131 billion operations per second!
2 The Wright brothers made the ... (early) powered flight in 1903.
3 What is the ... (good) gadget you have read about?
4 Archimedes invented some of the ... (effective) war machines.
5 The ... (old) mechanical clock (1335) is in Milan, Italy.
6 Atomic clocks are the ... (accurate).
7 One of the ... (famous) inventors is Thomas Edison.
8 The ... (long) bicycle is over 22 metres long!

B

Write sentences using *going to*.

Example: 1 They aren't going to send astronauts to Venus.

1 they / not / send astronauts to Venus
2 I / take my dog to the vet tonight
3 he / not / go to university
4 what time / we / meet?
5 she / take her driving test tomorrow
6 we / invite him to the party?
7 they / send me the money
8 you / take a camera?

Vocabulary

C

Match these machines and gadgets with why you use them.

vacuum cleaner TV remote control calculator smoke alarm photocopier microwave oven

1 to do calculations
2 to clean carpets
3 to detect the possibility of a fire
4 to change channels without getting up
5 to heat food quickly
6 to make copies of text or pictures

D

Match the verbs with the nouns.

1	play	**a**	time
2	cross	**b**	sport
3	waste	**c**	a problem
4	solve	**d**	fun
5	have	**e**	the road

Pronunciation: Difficult Words

E

Listen and repeat these words from the module:

artificial / athlete / expect / gadget / lipstick / precious / scientist / scratch / special / strangest

Machines

Module check

Grammar Reference

14 Superlatives

- **Remember!** Adjectives can be **short**, **long** or **irregular**.

- **Short**: 1 syllable, or 2 syllables that end in *y*:

adjective	superlative
strange	the strang**est**
big	the big**gest**
easy	the eas**iest**

- **Long**: 2 syllables that do not end in *y*, or more than 2 syllables:

adjective	superlative
dangerous	superiority: the **most dangerous**
	inferiority: the **least** dangerous

- **Irregular**: they change completely:

adjective	superlative
good	the **best**
bad	the **worst**

The silliest gadget is this portable zebra crossing.
Is hang-gliding **the most dangerous** sport?
This is **the worst** television programme I've ever watched.

15 Future with *going to*: affirmative, negative and interrogative

- The future with **going to** is used to describe plans for the future.

- It is formed with the present of **to be** + **going to** + the infinitive.

- Affirmative: **I'm going to learn** more English this summer.

- Negative: **She's not going to go out** so often.

- Interrogative: When **are you going to come** with us?

Keyword Check

Machines: computer, microwave oven, photocopier, vacuum cleaner, video player

Gadgets: automatic car-door opener, key-ring light, mobile phone, pocket calculator, pocket translator, smoke alarm, TV remote control

Transport: aeroplane, airship, car, hang-glider, helicopter, hot-air balloon, motorbike

Travel: exploration, flight, journey, passenger

Adjectives: amazing, artificial, dangerous, early, famous, modern, natural, popular, portable, practical, silly, strange, unusual, useful

Explaining: You need this because... / Basically, this invention is... / To solve this problem... / It is useful, so you can...

Can you add more words to these lists?

1 Look at Grammar References 14 and 15 on this page and complete Grammar File 8 in the Activity Book. Then do the *Test Yourself: Grammar* on page 60 of the Activity Book.

2 Look at the Keyword Check. Write important new words in your vocabulary book. Then do the *Test Yourself: Vocabulary* on page 60 of the Activity Book.

WELCOME TO

WORLD CLUB MAGAZINE!

In this magazine you can: read stories, do puzzles, play games and have fun!
You can also make your own magazine. This symbol  means:
Add this to your magazine! Good luck!!

Sports

Crossword

Tuna, Mayonnaise, Cheese and Banana Sandwich

Computer Game

Romance

1

Which one's the odd-one-out? Can you find the animal that is in the wrong group?

1 a) ant b) cockroach c) spider
2 a) eagle b) penguin c) ostrich
3 a) bat b) dolphin c) ant
4 a) chameleon b) snake c) crocodile
5 a) lion b) zebra c) tiger
6 a) hamster b) rabbit c) kiwi

 Now write your own animal "odd-one-out".

2

Animal Quiz

What do you know about chimps?

1 Chimpanzees come from:
   a Asia b Asia and Africa c Africa
2 Chimpanzees weigh:
   a 20 kilos b 30 kilos c 40 kilos
3 Chimpanzees eat:
   a fruit, insects and sometimes meat
   b insect and small animals c leaves
   and grass
4 Chimpanzees live:
   a in large groups b in small groups
   c individually

**Now read about chimpanzees.
Were you right?**

Sometimes we see chimpanzees doing human things. They drink from cups, or take photos. Why? Chimpanzees belong to the same family of apes as the huge gorillas of Africa and the red orang-utan of Southeast Asia, but scientists think the chimpanzees are the most intelligent.

They come from the rain forests and grasslands of Central and West Africa; they have got long black hair and they haven't got tails. An adult male is about 85 centimetres tall and weighs about forty kilos.

Chimpanzees live in large groups of twenty-five to fifty animals, and one male chimpanzee is the leader. They spend most of their time on the ground but they also climb trees to find food. They eat mainly fruit and insects, and sometimes they eat meat, such as monkeys. When they hunt, the males work together. Then they share the food with the whole family group.

But the greatest sign of the chimpanzee's intelligence is that it makes and uses tools. It pokes a stick into an ants' nest, then pulls out the stick and eats the ants. It also uses stones to crack nuts, and it chews leaves to make a sponge to mop up water. Some chimpanzees can even communicate with humans by using sign language or a computer!

3 Crossword

Mystery word

Can you do our animal crossword?

1   A very large bird that can't fly.
2   A tiger has got very ... claws.
3   A very small animal with six legs.
4   An animal which gives milk to its young.
5   A wild cat from North and South America,
6   A popular pet.
7   The elephant's nose.
8   An African animal like a horse but striped.
9   Camels can live in the ... .
10 Monkeys live in tropical ... .

The mystery word is: ...

 Now make up a similar puzzle, using words from Module 1.

• Choose a long word to go down.
• Find words to go across, using the letters in the long word.
• Write your clues. (The mini-dictionary may help you.)
• Copy out the puzzle with the clues and give it to your friends to do.

4 What goes where?!

Read about the flat and then try to name the rooms on the plan.

My brother and his wife live in a lovely little flat. They've got a beautiful living room with three big windows. They sit and watch TV in the living room and they eat there too because they haven't got a separate dining room. When you stand in the hall at the front door, the kitchen is on the right and the bedroom is in front of you. It's lovely because it's got a big balcony. There's a small bathroom between the kitchen and the bedroom.

 Draw a plan of a flat you like and write a description.

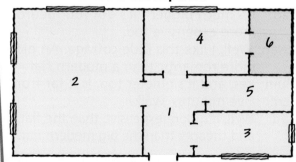

WORLD CLUB MAGAZINE!

Who's Who in Amanda's family?

Read about Amanda's family. Can you name her relatives?

This is a photo of my Aunt Vera's birthday party last month. That's her sitting opposite my grandfather. Next to Aunt Vera are my three little cousins: Ben, Jo and Sophie. At the end of the table is my Uncle Ted. In between Uncle Ted and my grandfather is my brother, Tim. And my grandmother is sitting opposite my cousin Ben. Can you see my brother's girlfriend, Lisa? She's sitting opposite my brother and she's talking to Uncle Ted.

Choose a holiday!

Ben's family want to plan their holiday. Which holiday house do they choose? Why?

Which do you prefer? Why?

A

B

C

Dad: So we don't want a hotel this year?

Mum: Well, it's cheaper to cook our own meals. You can all help with the cooking. Look, this is a nice little flat, and the village isn't a long way from the sea.

Ben: Why can't we be nearer the sea? I like this modern flat. Look, the building is next to the sea. We can go and swim before breakfast.

Dad: It's much bigger - it's got four bedrooms! It's much more expensive too.

Susan: Well, I like this little cottage. An old cottage is more romantic than a modern flat.

Mum: Yes, and it's quieter too. Is it far from the sea?

Ben: Five minutes' walk.

Dad: Well, it's more expensive than the flat in the village and cheaper than the big modern flat. OK. Let's take it.

Film Show

What kind of films are these? Invent titles for them.

A A French nuclear scientist disappears with a secret file. An exciting story which takes us from the Caribbean to Cairo, from Moscow to Madrid...

B More funny adventures with Hamish Minty about his life as a doctor in the islands of Scotland.

Now invent a title and a description of a film.

8

10

LEGENDS AND MYTHS

Can you match these legendary people to the clues in column 2?

1	2
i King Arthur	a Friday
ii Don Quijote	b Charles Dickens
iii Peter Pan	c Rocinante
iv Robin Hood	d Excalibur
v Robinson Crusoe	e Never never land
vi Oliver Twist	f Little John

Check your answers.

(id; iic; iiie; ivf; va; vib)

9

How confident are you in a romantic situation? Answer the questions and find out!

Romance questionnaire

1 When you like someone at your school, do you a) speak to him/her? b) phone him/her c) ask your friends about him/her?

2 When you like someone you see in the street, do you.. a) tell him/her you like him/her? b) look at him/her and smile? c) ask him/her the time?

3 At parties, do you a) start talking to people b) join a group of people? c) wait for people to talk to you?

4 When everybody is dancing at a disco, do you a) start dancing at once? b) ask somebody to dance with you? c) wait for somebody to ask you to dance?

5 When you meet someone nice on holiday, do you a) phone him/her? b) write a letter to him/her? c) wait for a letter from him/her?

6 When you want to go out with somebody, do you a) invite him/her to your house? b) invite him/her for a coke? c) wait for him/her to invite you?

 Add two more questions of your own. Then ask your friends to answer the questionnaire.

Score:

Mostly a) - You are a very confident person. Don't push yourself too much!

Mostly b) - You are good with people, not too confident, not too shy.

Mostly c) - You are a very shy person. Try to be more confident.

Look at this Web page about Nicolas Cage.

Back	Forward	Print	Fav

Site name

My favourite film star:
Nicolas Cage

Starred in:
Connair

Best film:
Honeymoon in Las Vegas

Born:
Nicolas Coppola, 7th January 1964 in Long Beach

TV début:
1982

Interesting fact:
He is the nephew of the famous film director Francis Ford Coppola.

 Design your own page about your favourite film star.

11 | POP QUIZ

How much do you know about rock and pop? Can you answer our pop quiz questions?

- What is the name of the hit album by the Backstreet Boys?
  a) The Year 2000 b) Millennium
  c) New Century
- Who is the lead guitarist of the Rolling Stones?
  a) Eric Clapton b) Keith Richard
  c) John Lennon
- Where does the singer Bjork come from?
  a) Iceland b) Sweden c) United States
- Who wrote the song 'Yesterday'?
  a) Bob Dylan b) John Denver
  c) Paul McCartney

 Now prepare a similar quiz for your friends.

12 | Sports

Where did these sports originally come from? Match the countries to the sports.

i	running	a	England
ii	chariot racing	b	China
iii	football	c	Greece
iv	hockey	d	Canada
v	lacrosse	e	The Roman Empire

Now read the text and check your answers

People have always enjoyed sports. In the early Olympic Games in Greece, about three thousand years ago, men ran in races. Then later, athletes also competed in jumping and throwing. The Romans loved chariot-racing, when men drove chariots with horses. And people crowded the stadium to watch men fighting - not boxing matches like today, but gladiators fighting each other or even wild animals.

Football began early too, perhaps over two thousand years ago in China. It became a popular sport all over the world. In England, hundreds of people played football together in two teams. Even with smaller teams it was a dangerous game. In 1863, rules were made to control the game. Rugby football, with different rules, began in 1823 when it was played at Rugby School in England.

Hockey is another game which began in England. Lacrosse, which was an American Indian game, first became popular in Canada. Cricket, the favourite summer game in England, began in the 16th century. At the same time, at the court of King Henry VIII, people played a kind of tennis, with racket and ball but indoors.

13

SPY QUIZ!

Imagine you are a spy. Answer this questionnaire and then check your results. Are you a good spy?

1 How many languages can you speak?
  a) one
  b) two
  c) more than two

2 Which of these things can you do?
  a) swim
  b) use a gun
  c) write in code
  d) do karate
  e) do judo
  f) follow people

3 Somebody is following you in the street. What do you do?
  a) Run very fast.
  b) Ask them why they are following you.
  c) Continue normally and tell your boss.

4 Enemy agents are interrogating you. What do you do?
  a) Say nothing and try to escape.
  b) Tell them everything.
  c) Invent a story.

Key: 1: a 0 b 1 c 2; 2: a 0 b 0 c 3 d 2 e 2 f 3; 3: a 0 b 0 c 3; 4: a 3 b 0 c 2

Scores: More than 15: A perfect spy!
10–15: A good spy. 5–10: OK.
Less than 5: look for an other job

14 Break the code!

You are a secret agent. You must take a briefcase to a certain place in Garuda City. Your instructions are in code. Work out the instructions, using the map on page 50.

Code

AZ	BY	CX	DW	EV	FU	GT
HS	IR	JQ	KP	LO	MN	NM
OL	PK	QJ	RI	SH	TG	UF
VE	WD	XC	YB	ZA		

Example: **TL LFG GO OUT**

**TL LFG LU XVMGIZO YFH
HGZGRLM ZMW GFIM IRTSG
DZOP FMWVI IZRODZB YIRWTV
GSVM GFIM OVUG TL RMGL
GSV KZIP LM GSV IRTSG
OVZEV YIRVUXZHV FMWVI
HVXLMW GIVV LM GSV OVUG**

 Now write a message in code for your friend.

15 Spot the Spy!

These three people work for the Atlanton government. Yesterday morning, some very important secret plans disappeared. Q is interrogating them to find out who stole them. Only one person was alone in the office and had a chance to get the plans. Who is the spy?

Miss Brown

'I arrived at the office at nine o'clock with Mr Green. We talked for about five minutes and then we started work. Mr White arrived late, at about ten o'clock, because he had to visit the doctor. At eleven o'clock, I went out of the office to take my report to the director. I talked to her for about twenty minutes and came back to the office at 11.25 a.m. I stayed in the office for another twenty five minutes and then I went out to have a coffee. I came back to the office after ten minutes. Finally I went for lunch half an hour after that.'

Mr White

'I arrived at ten o'clock and started to work immediately. I made several phone calls. I talked on the telephone for an hour. Then I spent twenty-five minutes typing a letter. I left the office to take the letter to another department. I was out of the office for half an hour. I came back to the office and I did some more work. I left at the same time as Miss Brown.'

Mr Green

'I arrived at the office at the same time as Miss Brown and we talked for five minutes. I worked on some secret plans for one and a half hours. Then I went out to have a coffee for fifteen minutes. After that I made a couple of phone calls and continued with the plans. I left the office at about half past twelve to have lunch.'

16 Recipe time - Tuna, Mayonnaise, Cheese and Banana Sandwich

Are you a good cook? Look at the pictures. Can you put the instructions for the recipe in the correct order?

Example: a = 5

Serves Four
Time Needed: *15 minutes*

Ingredients
175g tin of tuna
125g cheese
200g mayonnaise
1 banana
salt and pepper

Food from around the world

Do you know which countries the food in these pictures comes from?

     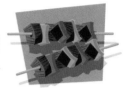 

Now read and check your answers.

Food is now international. We can eat burgers anywhere in the world today, but they started in the United States. The Americans were the first to produce 'fast food'. Pizza was an Italian recipe but it became popular in the United States and spread from there all over the world. 'French fries' is the American name for fried chipped potatoes which in England are called 'chips'.

Do you have Indian or Chinese restaurants where you live? In Chinese food, the meat, fish and vegetables are cut into small pieces and cooked very lightly. Indian food, on the other hand, is cooked slowly, with a lot of hot spices. Mexican food is very spicy too. The countries of the Eastern Mediterranean also like food with a strong taste. They gave us 'kebabs', pieces of meat cooked on long sticks, and many different kinds of salad.

What other national dishes do you know? English people still enjoy their 'fish and chips' which you can buy in a take-away and eat straight from the paper. In Spain, a 'paella' is a family favourite – a dish of rice with different kinds of seafood. And an Italian meal usually includes a dish of pasta with a delicious sauce.

If you can't travel to these countries, try a restaurant. If you can't do that, buy a recipe book and cook something different at home!

a) Cut the banana in pieces and put them in the bowl.

b) Open the tin of tuna.

c) Mix all the ingredients together. Add salt and pepper.

d) Put the tuna in a bowl and break it up with a fork.

e) Grate the cheese and add it to the tuna.

f) Put the mixture on a piece of bread or a roll. It is ready to eat!

g) Mix the mayonnaise with the tuna and cheese.

 Now write your own recipe for a sandwich. You can invent an unusual one if you like. Remember to include:

• ingredients   • instructions

18 HEALTHY LIVING?

Find out how healthy your diet is. In your notebook, make a list of what you ate yesterday and the day before.

	Yesterday	Day before
morning		
afternoon		
evening		
night		

You get one point for every healthy thing. Take away two points for every unhealthy thing. If your score is negative, you have to change your diet!

19 You're a winner!

Mike, Jane and Mark have all won a lot of money in a competition. What do you think they will do to celebrate? What will they buy? What kind of holiday will they choose? The ideas below may help you.

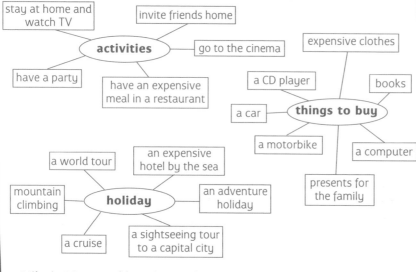

stay at home and watch TV · invite friends home · **activities** · go to the cinema · have a party · have an expensive meal in a restaurant · expensive clothes · a CD player · books · a car · **things to buy** · a motorbike · a computer · presents for the family · a world tour · an expensive hotel by the sea · mountain climbing · **holiday** · an adventure holiday · a cruise · a sightseeing tour to a capital city

Mike is 16 years old. He is a student. He loves cars and wants to learn how to drive. He also enjoys football. He doesn't like music much, but he likes going out to the cinema with his friends.

Jane is 17 years old. She finished school last year and is now working as a waitress. She likes going out with friends. She doesn't want to get married for a few years. She loves music. She wants to travel abroad. She likes foreign food and enjoys trying out different recipes.

Mark is 19 years old. He is studying computer science at university and he wants to start his own computer business. He is a very quiet person. He lives with his parents and he doesn't go out very often.

Imagine you win a lot of money. What do you think you will do? What won't you do? Why?

20 Word Wheel

Can you complete the word wheel?

1 A person who dances.
2 A person who works on a farm.
3 A person who works in a hospital.
4 A person who drives something.
5 A person who writes books.
6 A person who sings.
7 A person who works in a restaurant.
8 A woman who has children.
9 A man who has children.

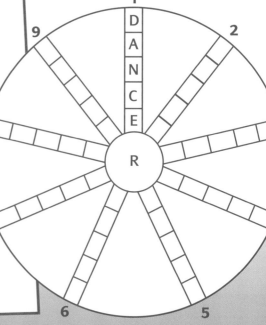

21 Computer Game

Read about the computer game and find out this information:

1 name of robots 2 location of base
3 levels in base 4 your task
5 assistance 6 obstacles

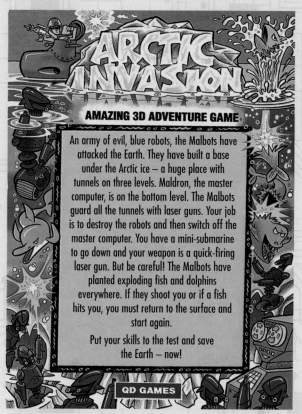

AMAZING 3D ADVENTURE GAME

An army of evil, blue robots, the Malbots have attacked the Earth. They have built a base under the Arctic ice – a huge place with tunnels on three levels. Maldron, the master computer, is on the bottom level. The Malbots guard all the tunnels with laser guns. Your job is to destroy the robots and then switch off the master computer. You have a mini-submarine to go down and your weapon is a quick-firing laser gun. But be careful! The Malbots have planted exploding fish and dolphins everywhere. If they shoot you or if a fish hits you, you must return to the surface and start again.

Put your skills to the test and save the Earth – now!

QD GAMES

Invent your own robot or alien computer game. Design an advertisement for the game. Describe the game and illustrate it.

22

Find one false statement in this aeroplane quiz.

1 The largest Zeppelin ever was the Hindenburg.
2 The first person ever to fly an aeroplane was Orville Jones in 1893.
3 The first person to fly an aeroplane solo and non-stop across the Atlantic was Charles Lindburgh.
4 Juan de la Cierva's 'autogiro', flown in 1923, was the first effective helicopter.
5 Concorde is the fastest commercial aeroplane.

number 2 is false, it was Orville Wright in 1903

23

Look at this invention. Give it a name, then prepare a brochure to advertise it. Include the following information:

No time to talk to your plants?

| Ten languages. | Special speakers for cactuses. | Use the revolutionary plant talker. |

24 Computer Counting

Computers use only two digits (1 and 0) to count. This is the binary system. Here is how it works:

Now answer the questions about Sam the robot.

1 How old is he?
2 How much does he cost?
3 How many jobs can he do?

DECIMAL	BINARY				
	(16)	(8)	(4)	(2)	(1)
0	0	0	0	0	0
1	0	0	0	0	1
2	0	0	0	1	0
3	0	0	0	1	1
4	0	0	1	0	0
5	0	0	1	0	1
10	0	1	0	1	0
25	1	1	0	0	1

Design your own robot and make notes about its age, price, how many jobs it can do and how long it takes to do them. Then make a poster including a picture and a description, using binary numbers.

Hi, my name's Sam. I'm new, I'm only 0110 months old. I can do 1100 different jobs in the house and my price is 1111 hundred pounds. Buy me now.

Mini-dictionary

This mini-dictionary will help you to understand all the words that are either important to remember or necessary to do the activities. Remember that you don't have to understand every word when you read a text. If you find a word in one of the texts which is not in the mini-dictionary then that word is not essential to do the activity. We recommend that you refer to the **Longman New Junior English Dictionary** (first published 1984) for words not included here. Remember that this mini-dictionary is not a substitute for a complete dictionary.

A

accurately / 'ækjʊrətli/ *adverb* correctly.

act /ækt/ *verb* 1 to do or behave: *The children* **acted** *very badly at school.* 2 to pretend to be someone else, in a play or a film.

act out /ˌækt aʊt/ *verb* perform: *We* **acted out** *our dialogue.*

actor / 'æktə/ *noun* a man who acts in plays or films.

actress / 'æktrɪs/ *noun* (plural **actresses**) a woman who acts in plays or films.

adventure /əd'ventʃə/ *noun* an exciting thing that happens to someone.

adventurous /əd'ventʃərəs/ *adjective* liking a life full of adventures.

advertisement /əd'vɜːtɪsmənt/ *noun* a notice or a short film offering something for sale: *a newspaper* **advertisement**, *an* **advertisement** *for a new soap.*

aeroplane / 'eərəpleɪn/ *noun* a large flying machine with wings, in which people can travel.

agreement /ə'griːmənt/ *noun* (no plural) having the same opinion as someone else.

aircraft / 'eəkrɑːft/ *noun* (plural **aircraft**) a flying machine.

airport / 'eəpɔːt/ *noun* a place where aircraft are kept and where they arrive and leave.

airship / 'eəʃɪp/ *noun* an old type of aircraft containing gas to make it lighter than air and with an engine to make it move.

album / 'ælbəm/ *noun* 1 a book with empty pages where you can put photographs, stamps, etc. 2 a record with several songs on each side: *a Corrs* **album**.

alien / 'eɪliən/ *noun* a creature from another world: *a spaceship full of* **aliens**.

alone /ə'ləʊn/ *adjective, adverb* not with other people: *He lives* **alone**.

along /ə'lɒŋ/ *preposition* following the length of: *We walked* **along** *the road.*

always / 'ɔːlweɪz/ *adverb* 1 at all times: *He* **always** *arrives late.* 2 for ever: *I shall* **always** *remember you.*

amazing /ə'meɪzɪŋ/ *adjective* very surprising and exciting: *What* **amazing** *news!*

ambitious /æm'bɪʃəs/ *adjective* wanting very much to be successful.

amusing /ə'mjuːzɪŋ/ *adjective* making you laugh or smile; funny: *an* **amusing** *story.*

ant /ænt/ *noun* a small insect that lives in large groups.

appear /ə'pɪə/ *verb* to come into sight: *He* **appeared** *on TV.*

appearance /ə'pɪərəns/ *noun* 1 the sudden arrival or coming into sight of a person or thing. 2 the way a person looks to other people: *his neat* **appearance**.

apple / 'æpəl/ *noun* a round, hard, juicy fruit which is usually red or green.

argue / 'ɑːgjuː/ *verb* to fight or disagree in words: *They often* **argued** *about money.*

article / 'ɑːtɪkəl/ *noun* 1 a thing: *an* **article** *of clothing.* 2 a piece of writing in a newspaper: *an* **article** *about ships.* 3 the words *a* or *an* (=indefinite article) or *the* (definite article).

artificial /ˌɑːtɪ'fɪʃəl/ *adjective* not real: **artificial** *flowers.*

artist / 'ɑːtɪst/ *noun* a person whose job is painting pictures.

ask /ɑːsk/ *verb* to say something that is a question: *"Who are you?" she* **asked**.

attach /ə'tætʃ/ *verb* to fix something to something else.

attractive /ə'træktɪv/ *adjective* pleasing, especially to look at.

automatic /ˌɔːtə'mætɪk/ *adjective* working by itself: **automatic** *doors* (= doors that open and close without being touched).

B

balcony / 'bælkəni/ *noun* (plural **balconies**) a place above the ground on the outside of a building where people can sit: *Our flat has a large* **balcony**.

banquet / 'bæŋkwɪt/ *noun* a special, important meal where there a lot of people.

base /beɪs/ *noun* 1 the bottom of something; the part that something stands on. 2 the place where something is controlled: *a military* **base**.

bat /bæt/ *noun* 1 a piece of wood for hitting the ball in some games: *a baseball* **bat**. 2 a small animal with wings that flies at night and hangs upside-down when it sleeps.

bathroom / 'bɑːθrʊm, -ruːm/ *noun* a room in a house where people wash their bodies or have baths.

bean /biːn/ *noun* a seed or seed container of a plant which is eaten as a vegetable: *green* **beans**.

bed /bed/ *noun* a piece of furniture you sleep on: *What time did you go to* **bed** *last night* (= go to your bed to sleep)?

bedroom / 'bedrʊm, -ruːm/ *noun* a room for sleeping in.

bee /biː/ *noun* a stinging, flying insect that makes honey.

before /bɪ'fɔː/ *preposition* earlier than: *You must leave* **before** *8 o'clock.*

bill /bɪl/ *noun* a piece of paper showing how much you must pay for something.

blind /blaɪnd/ *adjective* not able to see.

body / ˈbɒdi/ *noun* (plural **bodies**)
1 the whole of a person or animal. 2 the central part of person or animal, not the head, arms or legs.

bomb /bɒm/ *noun* a container full of material that will explode.

bone /bəʊn/ *noun* one of the hard white parts in a person's or an animal's body.

bookshelves / ˈbʊkʃelvz/ *noun* (plural) a piece of furniture with space for books.

boring / ˈbɔːrɪŋ/ *adjective* not interesting; dull: *a **boring** film.*

boss /bɒs/ *noun* a person who is in charge and tells other people what work to do.

bottom / ˈbɒtəm/ *noun* 1 the lowest part of something: *at the **bottom** of the page.* 2 the base of something: *The price is on the **bottom** of the box.* 3 the lowest position in something: *He's at the **bottom** of the class.*

bravery / ˈbreɪvəri/ *noun* (no plural) willingness to do dangerous things without feeling afraid.

bread /bred/ *noun* (no plural) a food made by mixing flour and water and then baking it: *a loaf of **bread**.*

break /breɪk/ *noun* 1 a short rest: *We have a **break** between lessons.* 2 an opening in something: *a **break** in the cable.* 3 a lucky chance: *This acting role was her big **break**.*

breakfast / ˈbrekfəst/ *noun* the first meal of the day.

briefcase / ˈbriːfkeɪs/ *noun* a thin flat case for carrying papers or books.

brilliant / ˈbrɪljənt/ *adjective* 1 very clever: *a **brilliant** idea, a **brilliant** student.* 2 something you say when you think something is very good: *The film was **brilliant**!*

bumblebee / ˈbʌmbəlbiː/ *noun* a large hairy bee that makes a loud noise when flying.

burn /bɜːn/ *verb* (past **burnt** /bɜːnt/ or **burned** /bɜːnd/) 1 to be on fire: *The house is **burning**.* 2 to damage or destroy something with fire: *We **burnt** the old furniture.* 3 to hurt yourself or a part of your body with something hot: *I've **burnt** my fingers.*

bus station / ˈbʌs ˌsteɪʃən/ *noun* a place where buses start and finish their journeys, and where people can get on and off.

bushbaby / ˈbʊʃˌbeɪbi/ *noun* (plural **bushbabies**) a small African animal with large eyes and ears, a long tail and long back legs for jumping.

business person / ˈbɪznɪs ˌpɜːsən/ *noun* a man or a woman who works in business, especially one who owns a company or helps to run it.

busy / ˈbɪzi/ *adjective* 1 working; not free; having a lot to do: *He is **busy** now. He's **busy** writing letters.* 2 full of activity: *a **busy** day, a **busy** street.*

C

cable / ˈkeɪbəl/ *noun* 1 a thick rope. 2 wires that carry electricity or telephone messages. 3 a message sent by cable.

cancer / ˈkænsə/ *noun* a serious illness in which a growth spreads in the body.

car /kɑː/ *noun* a vehicle on wheels, driven by an engine, that you can travel in.

carbohydrate /kɑːbəʊˈhaɪdreɪt, -drət/ *noun* a substance in food like bread, cakes, potatoes, etc. which gives the body heat and energy and makes you fat if you eat too much of it.

card /kɑːd/ *noun* 1 a piece of stiff thick paper with a picture on the front and a message inside: *a birthday **card**.* 2 a small piece of stiff paper with pictures and numbers used for various games.

carpenter / ˈkɑːpɪntə/ *noun* a person who makes things out of wood as a job.

carpet / ˈkɑːpɪt/ *noun* a large mat used to cover the floor.

carrot / ˈkærət/ *noun* a vegetable with a long orange root.

cathedral /kəˈθiːdrəl/ *noun* an important large church.

cave /keɪv/ *noun* a hollow place under the ground or in the side of a mountain.

century / ˈsentʃəri/ *noun* (plural **centuries**) a period of 100 years: *the twentieth **century**.*

CD player /siː diː ˌpleɪə/ *noun* a special machine for playing CDs.

celebrate / ˈseləbreɪt/ *verb* to show that you are happy about something by having a special meal or party.

cellar / ˈselə/ *noun* a room under the ground in a house, used especially for storing things in.

chameleon /kəˈmiːliən/ *noun* a small lizard which can change its colour to match its surroundings.

change /tʃeɪndʒ/ *verb* 1 to become or make different: *This town has **changed** since I was a child.* 2 to take or put something in the place of something else: *She took the dress back to the shop and **changed** it (for another).*

character / ˈkærɪktə/ *noun* 1 what a person or thing is like: *He has a strong but gentle **character**.* 2 a person in a book, film or play.

chart /tʃɑːt/ *noun* 1 a table showing information. 2 **the charts** (plural) a list of the most popular records.

cheap /tʃiːp/ *adjective* costing only a little money; not expensive.

cheese /tʃiːz/ *noun* a solid food made from milk.

cheetah / ˈtʃiːtə/ *noun* a large animal of the cat family, able to run very fast.

chicken / ˈtʃɪkən/ *noun* a bird kept by people for its eggs and meat: *We had **chicken** for dinner.*

chimpanzee /ˌtʃɪmpænziː, -pən-/ *noun* an African animal like a monkey but without a tail.

chocolate mousse /ˌtʃɒklɪt muːs/ *noun* a sweet dish made from cream, eggs, chocolate and other substances mixed together and then frozen.

classical / ˈklæsɪkəl/ *adjective* (used about music) serious and of lasting importance: *I prefer **classical** music to pop.*

claw /klɔː/ *noun* 1 one of the sharp, hard points on the foot of a bird or animal. 2 the hand of a crab or lobster.

clean /kliːn/ *verb* to make something free from dirt: *Have you **cleaned** the kitchen?*

cliff /klɪf/ *noun* an area of high steep rock, often close to the sea.

cobra / ˈkəʊbrə/ *noun* an African or Asian poisonous snake.

Mini-dictionary

cockroach / ˈkɒkrəʊtʃ/ *noun* a large black insect which usually appears at night time and likes kitchens.

code /kəʊd/ *noun* a way of using words, letters, numbers, etc. to keep messages secret: *The letter was written in* **code** *and I couldn't understand it.*

coffee / ˈkɒfi/ *noun* 1 (no plural) (a drink made from) a brown powder from the seeds of the coffee tree. 2 a cup of this drink: *Two* **coffees**, *please.*

come /kʌm/ *verb* (present participle **coming** / ˈkʌmɪŋ/, past tense **came** /keɪm/, past participle **come** /kʌm/) to move towards the person speaking: *"**Come** here, Mary. I want to speak to you."*
1 **come back** to return: *They* **came** *back from holiday yesterday.*
2 **come into** to enter.
3 **come out** to appear.

comedy / ˈkɒmədi/ *noun* (plural **comedies**) a funny play, film, etc.; something that makes us laugh.

communication /kəˌmjuːnɪˈkeɪʃən/ *noun* speaking or writing to someone and being understood by them.

computer /kəmˈpjuːtə/ *noun* a machine that can store information and work out answers quickly.

computer science /kəmˌpjuːtə saɪəns/ *noun* knowledge or study of computers.

concert / ˈkɒnsət/ *noun* music played in public for a lot of people.

confident / ˈkɒnfɪdənt/ *adjective* feeling sure or safe: *He is* **confident** *he has passed the exam.*

contact / ˈkɒntækt/ *noun* touching or coming together: *She comes into* **contact** *with many people.*

contract / ˈkɒntrækt/ *noun* a written agreement to do work or sell something.

convenient /kənˈviːniənt/ *adjective* suited to your needs.

cottage / ˈkɒtɪdʒ/ *noun* a small attractive house in the country.

courtyard / ˈkɔːtjɑːd/ *noun* an open space inside or in front of a large building.

crash /kræʃ/ *noun* 1 a loud noise, like something large falling over: *The car hit the tree with a* **crash**. 2 an accident when vehicles hit each other: *a car* **crash**.

creative /kriˈeɪtɪv/ *adjective* producing new and original ideas and things.

cross /krɒs/ *verb* to go over: *They* **crossed** *the road.*

cross over /ˌkrɒs əʊvə/ *verb* to go over the road: *They* **crossed over** *and went into the post office.*

cucumber / ˈkjuːkʌmbə/ *noun* a long thin green vegetable, usually eaten without cooking.

cupboard / ˈkʌbəd/ *noun* a piece of furniture with shelves and a door, in which you keep clothes, plates or food.

curtain / ˈkɜːtn/ *noun* a piece of cloth hung up to cover a window, door or part of a room.

cut /kʌt/ *verb* (present participle **cutting** / ˈkʌtɪŋ/, past tense **cut** /kʌt/, past participle **cut** /kʌt/) to break with a knife or blade: *He* **cut** *the apple in half. He has* **cut** *his leg. She* **cut** *her hair.*

cut off /ˌkʌt ɒf/ *verb* 1 to stop or disconnect something: *They've* **cut** *the gas* **off**. 2 to separate a part from the rest: *They* **cut off** *her head.*

cycling / ˈsaɪklɪŋ/ *noun* (no plural) the sport of riding a bicycle.

D

dangerous / ˈdeɪndʒərəs/ *adjective* likely to harm people: *a* **dangerous** *driver.*

delicious /dɪˈlɪʃəs/ *adjective* good to eat: *The soup is* **delicious**.

desert / ˈdezət/ *noun* a large, empty, usually very dry place where almost nothing grows.

design /dɪˈzaɪn/ *verb* to make a plan for something: *Who* **designed** *the new house?*

desk /desk/ *noun* a work-table, often with space inside it for keeping books, pens, etc.

dessert /dɪˈzɜːt/ *noun* a sweet dish that you eat at the end of a meal.

destroy /dɪˈstrɔɪ/ *verb* to break up or get rid of completely: *The fire* **destroyed** *all my books.*

detect /dɪˈtekt/ *verb* to discover: *A policeman* **detects** *criminals.*

diagnosis /ˌdaɪəgˈnəʊsɪs/ *noun* the act of finding out what is wrong and describing it: *The doctor's* **diagnosis** *was influenza.*

dinner / ˈdɪnə/ *noun* the largest meal of the day, eaten in the evening or the middle of the day.

director /dɪˈrektə, daɪ-/ *noun* a person who controls a business or a film.

dirty / ˈdɜːti/ *adjective* (**dirtier**, **dirtiest**) not clean.

disappointed /ˌdɪsəˈpɔɪntɪd/ *adjective* sad because something is not as good or as nice as you expected.

discovery /dɪsˈkʌvəri/ *noun* (plural **discoveries**) something found or learned for the first time: *a new* **discovery** *in medical science.*

domestic /dəˈmestɪk/ *adjective* 1 found in or to do with the home: **domestic** *jobs like cleaning and cooking.* 2 not wild: *Cows are* **domestic** *animals.*

doubledecker bus /ˌdʌbəlˌdekə bʌs/ *noun* a bus with two levels, downstairs and upstairs.

dove /dʌv/ *noun* a white bird, often used as a sign of peace.

downstairs /ˌdaʊnˈsteəz/ *adverb* in or towards the part of a house which is on the same level as the ground: *The bathroom is* **downstairs**.

dream /driːm/ *verb* (past **dreamt** /dremt/ or **dreamed** /driːmd/) 1 to imagine things while you are asleep: *I* **dreamt** *about my teacher last night.* 2 to imagine something nice: *I* **dream** *of being a pop star.*

drive /draɪv/ *verb* (present participle **driving** / ˈdraɪvɪŋ/, past tense **drove** /drəʊv/, past participle **driven** /ˈdrɪvən/) to make a vehicle move in the direction you want: **drive** *a car.*

drop /drɒp/ *verb* (present participle **dropping** /ˈdrɒpɪŋ/, past tense **dropped** /drɒpt/, past participle **dropped** /drɒpt/) to fall or let fall: *The plate* **dropped** *from her hands. She* **dropped** *the plate.*

drop /drɒp/ *noun* a small amount of liquid: *A few* **drops** *of rain landed on the roof.*

E

eagle / ˈiːgəl/ *noun* a large bird that kills other creatures for food.

early / ˈɜːli/ *adjective, adverb* (**earlier**, **earliest**) 1 before the usual or agreed time: *The bus arrived* **early**. 2 near the beginning of a day, year, etc.: *Do you get up* **early**?

earn /ɜːn/ *verb* to get money for work you do: *She* **earns** *a lot of money.*

earring / ˈɪərɪŋ/ *noun* a piece of jewellery you wear on your ear.

easy / ˈiːzi/ *adjective* (**easier, easiest**) not difficult; done with no trouble: *It was an* **easy** *job and we did it quickly.*

eco-house / ˈiːkəʊ ˌhaʊs/ *noun* a house designed following ecological ideas.

ecological /ˌiːkəˈlɒdʒɪkəl/ *adjective* relating to the natural relations of plants and animals with their surroundings.

economical /ˌekəˈnɒmɪkəl, ˌiː-/ *adjective* cheap: *Going by train is more* **economical** *than going by plane.*

egg /eg/ *noun* a rounded thing from which baby birds, snakes, fish or insects come: *We eat hens'* **eggs**.

electronic /ɪˌlekˈtrɒnɪk, ˌelɪk-/ *adjective* produced by or working by an electric current passing through chips, transistors or valves: **electronic** *music.*

embarrassed /ɪmˈbærəst/ *adjective* nervous or uncomfortable in front of other people.

embassy /ˈembəsi/ *noun* (plural **embassies**) a place where people work to represent their own country in another country.

enemy /ˈenəmi/ *noun* (plural **enemies**) a person or country that is not friendly to you or that wants to harm you: *The two countries are* **enemies**.

engine /ˈendʒɪn/ *noun* a machine which uses petrol, oil, gas, electricity or steam and which makes things move or work: *a car* **engine**.

engineer /ˌendʒɪˈnɪə/ *noun* a person who is trained to plan and build machines, roads, bridges, etc.

enjoy /ɪnˈdʒɔɪ/ *verb* to get pleasure from: *I* **enjoy** *my job.*

entertainment /ˌentəˈteɪnmənt/ *noun* (no plural) activities which amuse or interest people: *For* **entertainment** *they watch television.*

environment /ɪnˈvaɪərənmənt/ *noun* 1 the conditions of the Earth and of the society surrounding you: *Children need a happy home* **environment**. 2 the world of land, sea and air that you live in: *Cutting down too many trees destroys the* **environment**.

exciting /ɪkˈsaɪtɪŋ/ *adjective* able to make someone excited; not boring: **exciting** *news.*

expensive /ɪkˈspensɪv/ *adjective* costing a lot of money; not cheap.

exploration /ˌekspləˈreɪʃən/ *noun* a journey through a place to learn about it.

explore /ɪkˈsplɔː/ *verb* to find out about a place by travelling through it.

explorer /ɪkˈsplɔːrə/ *noun* a person who travels into an unknown area to find out about it.

F

fall /fɔːl/ *verb* (past tense **fell** /fel/, past participle **fallen** /ˈfɔːlən/) to drop to a lower place: *The price of food has* **fallen**. *The apples* **fell** *off the tree.*

fancy /ˈfænsi/ *verb* to have a desire for something: *I* **fancy** *an ice cream.*

fantasy /ˈfæntəsi/ *noun* something unreal that you imagine.

feather /ˈfeðə/ *noun* one of the things that cover birds.

female /ˈfiːmeɪl/ *adjective* belonging to the sex of a woman: **Female** *animals give birth to young ones.*

finally /ˈfaɪnəl-i/ *adverb* at the end: **Finally**, *bake the cake for 30 minutes.*

find /faɪnd/ *verb* (past **found** /faʊnd/) to see or get something after you have been looking for it: *I* **found** *my money in my bag.*

fire-fighting /ˈfaɪə ˌfaɪtɪŋ/ *noun* putting out fires.

fish /fɪʃ/ *noun* (plural **fish** or **fishes**) a cold-blooded animal that lives in water: *He ate* **fish** *and chips.*

flat /flæt/ *noun* apartment; a number of rooms on one floor of a building where a person or family lives.

flight /flaɪt/ *noun* a journey on a plane.

floor /flɔː/ *noun* 1 the part of a room you walk on: *a wooden* **floor**. 2 all the rooms on one level: *We live on the third* **floor**.

forest /ˈfɒrɪst/ *noun* an area where a lot of trees grow thickly together.

form /fɔːm/ *verb* to make: *We* **formed** *a club for people who liked cars.*

freedom /ˈfriːdəm/ *noun* (no plural) being able to do what you want without being a prisoner and without being under another person's control.

fresh /freʃ/ *adjective* 1 picked, killed, etc. a short time ago: *These vegetables are* **fresh**. 2 pleasantly cool: *The air was* **fresh** *after the rain.*

fried /fraɪd/ *adjective* cooked in hot oil: **fried** *eggs.*

fruit /fruːt/ *noun* (plural **fruit**) the part of a plant which carries the seeds; it is often sweet and good to eat: *Would you like some* **fruit** *- an apple or an orange?*

fur /fɜː/ *noun* (no plural) the soft hair on some animals, like rabbits and cats.

furniture /ˈfɜːnɪtʃə/ *noun* (no plural) things used in a house, like beds, tables and chairs.

G

gadget /ˈgædʒɪt/ *noun* a small machine or useful apparatus.

garden /ˈgɑːdn/ *noun* a piece of land where trees, flowers or vegetables are grown, round a house or in a public place.

get /get/ *verb* (past **got** /gɒt/) 1 to take, have or buy: *I* **got** *a letter from Maria this morning. I must* **get** *some fruit in the market. I have* **got** *a dog.* 2 to become: *I* **got** *angry with him.* 3 to arrive: *We* **got** *to the station early.*

1 **get off** to leave a public vehicle: *I* **got off** *the bus.*

2 **get on** 1 to seat oneself on something: *He* **got on** *his bike.* 2 to enter a public vehicle: *She* **got on** *the train.*

3 **get up** to rise from a lying or sitting position: *He* **got up** *from the chair. I* **get up** *early in the morning.*

giant panda /ˌdʒaɪənt ˈpændə/ *noun* (or **panda**) a large animal like a bear, with black and white fur, originally from China.

go /gəʊ/ *verb* (past tense **went** /went/, past participle **gone** /gɒn/) 1 to move towards a place: *She* **went** *into the kitchen.* 2 to leave a place: *The train* **goes** *in five minutes.* 3 to travel somewhere, usually to do something: *They've* **gone** *shopping.*

1 **go in** or **into** to enter.

2 **go out** or **out of** to leave a building.

3 **go straight on** to continue without turning left or right.

gold /gəʊld/ *noun* (no plural) a yellow metal that costs a lot of money: *She wore a* **gold** *ring.*

golden /ˈgəʊldən/ *adjective* like or made of gold: **golden** *hair.*

good-looking /ˌgʊd ˈlʊkɪŋ/ *adjective* (used about a person) attractive: *He's very* **good-looking**.

gorgeous /ˈgɔːdʒəs/ *adjective* very nice or beautiful.

government /ˈgʌvəmənt, (ˈgʌvənmənt)/ *noun* the people who control what happens in a country.

grain /greɪn/ *noun* (no plural) a crop like wheat, maize or rice that has seeds which we eat.

grass /grɑːs/ *noun* (no plural) a plant with thin leaves that covers fields and gardens: *We sat on the* **grass** *to have our picnic.*

grasshopper / ˈgrɑːsˌhɒpə/ *noun* an insect with strong back legs for jumping.

group /gruːp/ *noun* 1 a number of people or things together: *a **group** of girls.* 2 a small number of people who sing and play pop music together.

grow /grəʊ/ *verb* (past tense **grew** /gruː/, past participle **grown** /grəʊn/) 1 to get bigger: *Children **grow** quickly.* 2 to care for plants and help them to get bigger: *I am **growing** an orange tree.*

grow up to change from being a child to a man or woman.

gymnastics /dʒɪmˈnæstɪks/ (also **gym**) *plural noun* exercises for your body that make you strong and able to move easily.

H

habitat / ˈhæbɪtæt/ *noun* the place where a plant or animal usually lives.

hall /hɔːl/ *noun* 1 the room just inside the front door of a house. 2 a large room or building: *The children were in the school **hall**.*

hang-glider / ˈhæŋˌglaɪdə/ *noun* a type of large kite which you hang from and use to fly through the air.

haunted / ˈhɔːntɪd/ *adjective* inhabited by ghosts: *a **haunted** house.*

head /hed/ *noun* 1 the top part of your body, where your brain, eyes, ears and mouth are. 2 someone who is in charge of a group of people.

heat /hiːt/ *verb* to make something hot: *We **heated** the soup on the cooker.*

health /helθ/ *noun* (no plural) the state of your body; how you are: *His **health** is not good (=he is often ill).*

hear /hɪə/ *verb* (past **heard** /hɜːd/) to notice sounds through your ears: *I **heard** the rain on the roof.*

helicopter / ˈhelɪkɒptə/ *noun* a flying machine with blades which go round on its top.

helpful / ˈhelpfʊl/ *adjective* doing something to help someone else: *She's so kind and **helpful**.*

hero / ˈhɪərəʊ/ *noun* (plural **heroes**) a man who does something great or brave: *Pele was Paul's **hero** when he was at school.*

heroine / ˈherəʊɪn/ *noun* a woman who does something great or brave.

hide /haɪd/ *verb* (past tense **hid** /hɪd/, past participle **hidden** /ˈhɪdn/) to put in a place not known to other people: *Where did you **hide** the money? I **hid** behind the door so no one would see me.*

historical /hɪˈstɒrɪkəl/ *adjective* in or about the past: *a **historical** film.*

hold /həʊld/ *verb* (past **held** /held/) 1 to have in the hand: *She is **holding** a book.* 2 to have inside: *This bottle **holds** one litre.*

hope /həʊp/ *verb* to want something to happen and to think it probably will happen: *I **hope** to go to college.*

horror / ˈhɒrə/ *noun* great fear and shock: *I watched the car crash in **horror**.*

hot-air balloon /hɒt eə bəˌluːn/ *noun* a bag of strong light material filled with gas or hot air so that it can float in the air, and carrying people in a basket.

human / ˈhjuːmən/ *adjective* of or like a person: *We are all **human** beings.*

I

igloo / ˈɪgluː/ *noun* a dome-shaped house built by Inuit people from blocks of icy snow.

ill /ɪl/ *adjective* not feeling healthy; unwell: *She can't go to school because she's **ill**.*

illegal /ɪˈliːgəl/ *adjective* not allowed by law: *It is **illegal** to steal things.*

illness / ˈɪlnɪs/ *noun* a disease: *to have an **illness**.*

insect / ˈɪnsekt/ *noun* a very small animal that has six legs: *Ants and bees are **insects**.*

instrument / ˈɪnstrəmənt/ *noun* 1 a tool used for doing a particular thing: *A pen is an **instrument** for writing.* 2 an object used for making music: *A piano is a musical **instrument**.*

intelligent /ɪnˈtelɪdʒənt/ *adjective* quick to learn and understand things; clever.

interplanetary /ˌɪntəˈplænətəri/ *adjective* happening or done between the planets: *interplanetary travel.*

interview / ˈɪntəvjuː/ *noun* a meeting to decide if a person is suitable for a job: *to go for an **interview**.*

invade /ɪnˈveɪd/ *verb* to attack and go into someone's land, house, etc.: *The army **invaded** the town.*

invent /ɪnˈvent/ *verb* to think of and plan something completely new: *Who **invented** the telephone?*

invention /ɪnˈvenʃən/ *noun* something completely new that has just been thought of and made: *This machine is their latest **invention**.*

isolated / ˈaɪsəleɪtɪd/ *adjective* far from other houses, towns, etc.: *an **isolated** house.*

isolation /ˌaɪsəˈleɪʃən/ *noun* (no plural) loneliness; being separate or far away.

J

job /dʒɒb/ *noun* 1 a piece of work that must be done: *My mother does all the **jobs** about the house.* 2 work that you are paid to do: *"What is your **job**?" "I'm a teacher."*

joke /dʒəʊk/ *noun* something you say or do to make people laugh: *Our teacher told us a **joke** today.*

journey / ˈdʒɜːni/ *noun* a trip, usually a long one: *How long is the **journey** to the coast?*

jump /dʒʌmp/ *verb* to move the body off the ground, up in the air or over something: *She **jumped** up onto the chair. The dog **jumped** over the gate.*

K

keep /kiːp/ *verb* (past **kept** /kept/) 1 to have or hold something: *Will you **keep** this book until next week and give it back to me then?* 2 to store something in a place: *Always **keep** your money in a safe place.*

keep on to continue: *He **kept** on walking.*

ketchup / ˈketʃəp/ *noun* (no plural) a thick red liquid made from tomatoes for flavouring food: *I like tomato **ketchup** on my chips.*

key-ring / ˈkiː rɪŋ/ *noun* a ring on which you can keep keys.

kid /kɪd/ *noun* 1 a child. 2 a young goat.

king /kɪŋ/ *noun* a male ruler of a country, especially one who comes from a family of rulers.

kitchen / ˈkɪtʃən/ *noun* a room used for cooking.

koala /kəʊˈɑːlə/ *noun* an Australian animal like a small bear.

Komodo dragon /kəˌməʊdəʊ ˈdrægən/ *noun* a very large lizard from the island of Komodo in Indonesia.

L

large /lɑːdʒ/ *adjective* big; able to hold a lot: *They need a **large** house because they have nine children.*

laser /'leɪzə/ *noun* an apparatus with a very strong, narrow beam of light used to cut metal, etc.

laugh /lɑːf/ *verb* to make a sound that shows you are pleased, happy, or think something is funny: *It was so funny we couldn't stop **laughing**.*

lay /leɪ/ *verb* (past **laid** /leɪd/) 1 to put down; to put in a certain place: **Lay** *the book on the table.* 2 to make eggs and send them out of the body: *The hen **laid** three eggs.*

leaf /liːf/ *noun* (plural **leaves** /liːvz/) one of the green flat parts of a plant or tree which grow out of branches or stems: *Some plants have **leaves** that grow straight out of the ground.*

leave /liːv/ *verb* (past **left** /left/) 1 to go away from a place or person: *The train **leaves** in five minutes. She **left** Australia for Britain.* 2 to let a thing stay in a place: *I **left** the books at home.*

lemon /'lemən/ *noun* a yellow fruit with a sour taste which grows on trees in hot places.

leopard /'lepəd/ *noun* a big cat with a spotted coat which lives in Africa and Asia.

lettuce /'letəs/ *noun* a vegetable with large soft green leaves which are eaten without cooking.

liberty /'lɪbəti/ *noun* (no plural) the state in which you are free and do not have to do what other people order: *They fought for their **liberty**.*

lift /lɪft/ *noun* a machine that carries people or things between floors of a tall building.

lighthouse /'laɪthaʊs/ *noun* a tall building with a strong light on top to guide boats or to tell them that they are near dangerous rocks.

living room /'lɪvɪŋ rʊm, ruːm/ *noun* the main room in a house where people can do things together, apart from eating.

lizard /'lɪzəd/ *noun* an animal with four short legs which has skin like a snake.

location /ləʊ'keɪʃən/ *noun* place or position.

long /lɒŋ/ *adjective* 1 measuring a great distance or time: *I take a **long** time to walk to school because it's a **long** way.* 2 measuring distance or time from one end to the other: *How **long** is the string? It's 30 centimetres **long**.*

look /lʊk/ *verb* to point the eyes towards a thing to try to see it: *I **looked** but I couldn't see the bird.*
1 **look after** to take care of someone or something: *She **looked after** my dog while I was on holiday.*
2 **look at** watch: *We **looked at** the blackboard.*
3 **look for** to try to find someone or something: *I'm **looking for** my key.*

luck /lʌk/ *noun* (no plural) the good and bad things that happen to you by chance: *It was good **luck** that I met you here; I did not expect to see you.*

lunch /lʌntʃ/ *noun* the meal that you eat in the middle of the day.

lyrics /'lɪrɪks/ *plural noun* the words of a popular song.

M

machine /mə'ʃiːn/ *noun* an instrument made up of many parts, used to do work: *A sewing **machine** helps us to sew things more quickly.*

male /meɪl/ *noun* a person or animal of the sex that does not give birth to young ones: *Men and boys are **males**.*

mammal /'mæməl/ *noun* an animal that is fed on its mother's milk when it is young, for example, a cow, a lion or a human baby.

mansion /'mænʃən/ *noun* a very large house.

marsupial /mɑː'suːpiəl, -'sjuː-/ *noun* a type of animal which carries its young in a pouch of skin on the mother's body.

mask /mɑːsk/ *noun* a covering over all or part of someone's face: *We all wore **masks** at the party and no one knew who we were.*

match /mætʃ/ *noun* a game between two people or two teams: *a football **match**.*

mayonnaise /ˌmeɪə'neɪz/ *noun* (no plural) a thick yellow sauce eaten with salads and other cold food.

meet /miːt/ *verb* (past **met** /met/) to come together: *I **met** my teacher in the street today.*

meeting /'miːtɪŋ/ *noun* a gathering of people to discuss something: *Many people came to the **meeting** in the hall.*

memorable /'memərəbəl/ *adjective* special and worth remembering.

menu /'menjuː/ *noun* a list of food that you can choose to eat in a restaurant, etc.

message /'mesɪdʒ/ *noun* news or an order sent from one person to another: *I have sent a **message** to tell her I shall be home late.*

microlight /'maɪkrəʊlaɪt/ *noun* a very small, light, low-speed aircraft with an open frame.

microwave oven /ˌmaɪkrəweɪv ʌvən/ *noun* an oven that uses microwaves to heat food.

military /'mɪlɪtəri/ *adjective* of soldiers: *a **military** hospital.*

milk /mɪlk/ *noun* (no plural) the white liquid that comes from female animals as food for their young: *We drink cows' **milk**.*

mineral water /'mɪnərəl ˌwɔːtə/ *noun* (no plural) a type of water that comes from under the ground that is sometimes put in bottles and sold to people as a drink.

mirror /'mɪrə/ *noun* a flat piece of glass with a shiny back in which you can see yourself.

missile /'mɪsaɪl/ *noun* an explosive weapon which can fly under its own power and which can be aimed at a distant object.

mission /'mɪʃən/ *noun* an important task given to someone by another person: *They gave him a secret **mission**.*

mobile phone /ˌməʊbaɪl fəʊn/ *noun* a telephone that you can carry with you wherever you go.

modern /'mɒdn/ *adjective* new, in the style that is popular now: **modern** *clothes,* **modern** *music.*

moon /muːn/ *noun* the large round thing that shines in the sky at night.

motorbike /'məʊtəbaɪk/ *noun* a large heavy bicycle worked by an engine.

motor racing /'məʊtə ˌreɪsɪŋ/ *noun* a sport where cars compete to drive the fastest.

mustard /'mʌstəd/ *noun* yellow powder made from the seeds of a plant, used mixed with water to give a hot taste to food.

N

nasty /'nɑːsti/ *adjective* (**nastier**, **nastiest**) not pleasant: **nasty** *medicine.*

natural /'nætʃərəl/ *adjective* not made by people or machines: *Cotton is a **natural** fabric.*

Mini-dictionary

nearly /'nɪəli/ *adverb* almost; not completely: *We have **nearly** finished.*

need /ni:d/ *verb* to want something that is necessary: *She **needs** some water because she is very thirsty.*

nervous /'nɜ:vəs/ *adjective* worried or afraid: *She's nervous about travelling alone.*

net /net/ *noun* 1 (no plural) material with open spaces between knotted thread, string or wire. 2 a piece of this material used for a particular purpose: *a football **net**, a fishing **net**.*

never /'nevə/ *adverb* not at any time; not ever: *I'll **never** forget her kindness.*

news broadcast /'nju:z ,brɔ:dkɑ:st/ *noun* a radio or television programme that gives information about things that have just happened.

next /nekst/ *adverb* just after something else: *What did he do **next**?*

next to /'nekst tə, tʊ/ *preposition* beside: *Come and sit **next to** me.*

noisy /'nɔɪzi/ *adjective* (**noisier, noisiest**) making a lot of loud, unpleasant sounds.

nose /nəʊz/ *noun* the part of the face through which we breathe and with which we smell.

nuclear /'nju:kliə/ *adjective* concerned with or using the very great power made by splitting an atom or joining atoms: **nuclear** *power*

nut /nʌt/ *noun* the dried fruit of a tree, with a hard shell.

O

observatory /əb'zɜ:vətəri/ *noun* (plural **observatories**) a place from where scientists can watch the moon, stars and the weather.

old /əʊld/ *adjective* 1 not young: *an **old** man.* 2 not new: **old** *clothes, an **old** building.*

onion /'ʌnjən/ *noun* a round vegetable with a strong smell, which is made up of one skin inside another and is often used in cooking.

operation /,ɒpə'reɪʃən/ *noun* a planned activity: *rescue **operations**.*

operations room /,ɒpə'reɪʃənz rʊm, ru:m/ *noun* the room where a military campaign is organised.

orange /'ɒrəndʒ/ *noun* a round sweet juicy fruit from the orange tree.

orange juice /ɒrəndʒ dʒu:s/ *noun* 1 the liquid that comes out of an orange. 2 a glass, cup or can of this liquid: *He bought an **orange juice**.*

ostrich /'ɒstrɪtʃ/ *noun* a very large bird with long legs which is black and white and cannot fly.

overnight /,əʊvə'naɪt/ *adverb* for the whole night: *We stayed **overnight** with my sister.*

P

palace /'pæləs/ *noun* a large beautiful building in which a king or other important person lives.

part /pɑ:t/ *noun* 1 some of a thing or things, but not all of it or them: *Which **part** of the town do you live in?* 2 a character played by an actor in a play or film: *He played the **part** of the soldier.*

party /'pɑ:ti/ *noun* (plural **parties**) a gathering at which people enjoy themselves, eat, drink, etc.: *a birthday **party**.*

passage /'pæsɪdʒ/ *noun* a narrow way in a building which connects different rooms: *The bathroom is at the end of the **passage**.*

passenger /'pæsɪndʒə/ *noun* a person who rides in a car, bus, train, etc. but does not drive it: *There were ten **passengers** in the bus.*

past /pɑ:st/ *preposition* up to and beyond: *He drove **past** the school but he didn't stop.*

pasta /'pæstə/ *noun* an Italian food made from flour and water, and often eaten with a sauce.

pension /'penʃən/ *noun* money given regularly to a person by their employer or the government when they are too old to work.

pepper /'pepə/ *noun* 1 (no plural) a powder made from the seeds of some plants and used to give food a hot taste. 2 the fruit of pepper plants, which can be eaten raw or used in cooking.

perform /pə'fɔ:m/ *verb* to do something to amuse or entertain people in a play, concert, etc.: *They're **performing** a new play tonight.*

petrol /'petrəl/ *noun* a liquid used in cars to make the engine work.

photo story /'fəʊtəʊ ,stɔ:ri/ *noun* a story told in a set of photos.

photocopier /'fəʊtəʊ,kɒpiə/ *noun* a special machine which makes photographic copies of pieces of writing.

piano /pi'ænəʊ/ *noun* a large musical instrument that you play by pressing small black and white bars.

picnic /'pɪknɪk/ *noun* a meal eaten outside, when you are away from home: *We had a **picnic** by the sea.*

pick up /,pɪk ʌp/ *verb* to take hold of something and lift it up: **Pick up** *your toys and put them in the cupboard.*

piranha /pɪ'rɑ:nə, -nə/ *noun* a fierce South American river fish that eats meat.

pizza /'pi:tsə/ *noun* a round flat piece of dough covered with cheese and other foods and then baked.

planet /'plænɪt/ *noun* one of the large masses like the Earth that go round a sun.

platypus /'plætɪpəs/ *noun* a small furry Australian animal that has a beak and feet like a duck's, lays eggs, and gives milk to its young.

player /'pleɪə/ *noun* a person who plays a game or a sport: *a tennis player.*

pocket /'pɒkɪt/ *noun* a piece of material sewn onto clothes to make a little bag to keep things in.

pocket calculator /,pɒkɪt kælkjʊleɪtə/ *noun* a small machine that you can use to add, subtract, etc, and which is small enough to go in your pocket.

pocket translator /,pɒkɪt træns'leɪtə, trænz-/ *noun* a small machine that you can use to translate words from one language to another, and which is small enough to go in your pocket.

polar bear /,pəʊlə beə/ *noun* a large white bear that lives near the North Pole.

pollution /pə'lu:ʃən/ *noun* (no plural) substances that make the air, water or soil dirty or dangerous: *The air in big cities is full of **pollution**.*

popular /'pɒpjʊlə/ *adjective* liked by many people: *This music is **popular** at the moment.*

portable /'pɔ:təbəl/ *adjective* quite small, light and easy to move or carry: *a **portable** computer.*

post office /'pəʊst ,ɒfɪs/ *noun* a place where you can buy stamps, post parcels, etc.

poster /'pəʊstə/ *noun* a large printed picture or paper put up on a wall, often advertising something.

potato /pə'teɪtəʊ/ *noun* (plural **potatoes**) a vegetable found under the ground and cooked before eaten.

pouch /paʊtʃ/ *noun* a pocket of skin in which kangaroos and other animals carry their young.

practical / ˈpræktɪkəl/ *adjective* good at doing things with your hands: *He is very* **practical** - *he can mend almost anything.*

primitive / ˈprɪmɪtɪv/ *adjective* early in human history: **Primitive** *people lived in caves.*

princess /prɪnˈses/ *noun* the daughter of a king and queen, or the wife of a prince.

problem / ˈprɒbləm/ *noun* something difficult or worrying: *We must solve this* **problem**.

promise / ˈprɒmɪs/ *verb* to say that you will certainly do something: *She* **promised** *to write a letter.*

protein / ˈprəʊtiːn/ *noun* a substance in food which helps to build the body: *Meat is a good source of* **protein**.

public transport /ˌpʌblɪk trænspɔːt/ *noun* a system of buses, trains, etc. for everyone to use.

puma / ˈpjuːmə/ *noun* a large member of the cat family which lives in North and South America.

put /pʊt/ *verb* (past **put** /pʊt/) to move to a place; to place: *He put the cups on the table.*

Q

quiet / ˈkwaɪət/ *adjective* not noisy; not loud.

R

racket / ˈrækɪt/ *noun* an instrument used to hit the ball in games like tennis.

rain /reɪn/ *noun* (no plural) water falling from the sky: *There was* **rain** *in the night.*

rat /ræt/ *noun* a small animal like a mouse but larger, which often eats food or grain that is stored.

reach /riːtʃ/ *verb* to get to a place or arrive at a place: *They* **reached** *London on Thursday.*

read /riːd/ *verb* (past **read** /red/) to look at words and understand them: *He* **read** *the story to his son.*

receive /rɪˈsiːv/ *verb* to get something or be given something: *Did you* **receive** *my letter?*

record /rɪˈkɔːd/ *verb* to store sounds electronically so that they can be listened to later: *He* **recorded** *his most popular songs in 1991.*

record / ˈrekɔːd/ *noun* a round thin flat piece of plastic that stores sounds, and which you play on a special machine.

remember /rɪˈmembə/ *verb* to keep in the mind; not to forget: *Did you* **remember** *to feed the animals?*

remote control /rɪˌməʊt kənˈtrəʊl/ *noun* a special thing you use to turn a machine on and off without getting out of your chair and going to it.

repair /rɪˈpeə/ *verb* to make something that is old or broken good again: *Have you* **repaired** *the chair yet?*

report /rɪˈpɔːt/ *noun* facts told or written: *The newspaper* **report** *was on the front page.*

reptile / ˈreptaɪl/ *noun* a cold-blooded animal such as a snake, a lizard, a crocodile, etc.

rescue / ˈreskjuː/ *noun* the saving of someone from danger: **rescue** *operations.*

revolting /rɪˈvəʊltɪŋ/ *adjective* making you ill through looking at or thinking about something: *What a* **revolting** *smell!*

rhythm / ˈrɪðəm/ *noun* a regular sound like a drum in music: *I can't dance to music without a good* **rhythm**.

ring /rɪŋ/ *noun* a circular metal band that you wear on your finger: *a wedding ring.*

robot / ˈrəʊbɒt/ *noun* a machine that does some of the work a person can do.

rocket / ˈrɒkɪt/ *noun* a thing driven into the air by burning gas, used to lift a weapon or a spaceship from the ground.

romantic /rəʊˈmæntɪk, rə-/ *adjective* showing strong feelings of love.

run /rʌn/ *verb* (present participle **running** / ˈrʌnɪŋ/, past tense **ran** /ræn/, past participle **run** /rʌn/) 1 to move quickly: *He* **ran** *across the road.* 2 to work or make work: *This machine is not* **running** *correctly.*

S

sad /sæd/ *adjective* unhappy.

safe /seɪf/ *adjective* not dangerous or harmful: 1 *This town is very* **safe** *at night.* 2 not in danger: *Will you be* **safe** *travelling by yourself?*

safety / ˈseɪfti/ *noun* (no plural) a safe place: *They escaped and ran to* **safety**.

salmon / ˈsæmən/ *noun* (plural **salmon**) a large river and sea fish that you can eat.

salt /sɔːlt/ *noun* (no plural) a white chemical found in sea-water, rocks, etc. which you can put on food to make it taste better.

sandwich / ˈsænwɪdʒ/ *noun* two pieces of bread put together with something else in between them: *I made a chicken* **sandwich**.

sardine /sɑːˈdiːn/ *noun* a small fish that is usually put into tins and used for food.

satellite / ˈsætəlaɪt/ *noun* an object sent into space to receive signals from one part of the world and send them to another: *The TV broadcast came from America by* **satellite**.

say /seɪ/ *verb* (past **said** /sed/) to speak something: *"I'm going to town,"* he **said**.

scan /skæn/ *verb* to read or examine something on a scanning machine.

science / ˈsaɪəns/ *noun* the study of nature and the way things in the world are made, behave, etc: *The main* **sciences** *are chemistry, physics and biology.*

science fiction /ˌsaɪəns fɪkʃən/ *noun* (no plural) stories about the future, life on other planets, etc.

scientist / ˈsaɪəntɪst/ *noun* a person who studies or practises science.

scratch /skrætʃ/ *verb* to make marks with something sharp: *The stick* **scratched** *the side of the car.*

script /skrɪpt/ *noun* a written form of a play, film, etc: *a film script.*

sea /siː/ *noun* the salt water that covers much of the Earth's surface.

secret / ˈsiːkrɪt/ *adjective* not known about by other people: *a secret message, secret plans.*

secret agent /ˌsiːkrɪt eɪdʒənt/ *noun* a person who secretly gathers information for a foreign government.

secret service /ˌsiːkrɪt sɜːvɪs/ *noun* the secret government department which tries to find out the secrets of enemy countries.

see /siː/ *verb* (past tense **saw** /sɔː/, past participle **seen** /siːn/) to use your eyes to know something: *It's dark in here; I can't* **see** *anything.*

send /send/ *verb* (past **sent** /sent/) to cause a thing to go somewhere: *She* **sent** *me a present.*

set /set/ *verb* (past **set** /set/) to put in a certain time and place: *The film is* **set** *in the past.*

several / ˈsevərəl/ *adjective* more than two, but not many: *She has* **several** *friends in the town.*

sharp /ʃɑːp/ *adjective* 1 having an edge that cuts easily: *a* **sharp** *knife.* 2 having a fine point: *a* **sharp** *pencil.*

shield /ʃiːld/ *noun* a piece of wood or metal that soldiers used to hold in front of them to protect their bodies in battle.

shy /ʃaɪ/ *adjective* nervous or afraid to be with other people: *The child was* **shy** *and hid behind his mother.*

sign /saɪn/ *verb* to write your name, for example at the end of a letter.

signal /ˈsɪɡnəl/ *noun* a movement or thing which tells you what to do: *The railway* **signal** *showed that the train could pass.*

silly /ˈsɪli/ *adjective* (**sillier, silliest**) not reasonable or clever: *Don't be* **silly***! That insect can't hurt you.*

sing /sɪŋ/ *verb* (past tense **sang** /sæŋ/, past participle **sung** /sʌŋ/) to make music with your voice: *She* **sang** *a song.*

singer /ˈsɪŋə/ *noun* a person who sings.

size /saɪz/ *noun* how big something or someone is: *What* **size** *is your house?*

smoke alarm /ˈsməʊk əˌlɑːm/ *noun* a thing which gives a warning that something is burning.

snout /snaʊt/ *noun* the long nose of animals like pigs.

sofa /ˈsəʊfə/ *noun* a long soft chair for two or more people to sit on: *sitting on the* **sofa** *in front of the television.*

solve /sɒlv/ *verb* to find the answer to something: *to solve a puzzle.*

song /sɒŋ/ *noun* a piece of music with words that are sung.

space shuttle /ˈspeɪs ˌʃʌtl/ *noun* a type of spaceship that can leave the Earth to travel in space and then return to the Earth again.

space station /ˈspeɪs ˌsteɪʃən/ *noun* a satellite used as a base for operations in space.

spaceship /ˈspeɪsʃɪp/ *noun* a vehicle that can carry people through space.

special effects /ˌspeʃəl ɪˈfekts/ *plural noun* (in film and television) special lighting, sound, camerawork and computer graphics: *The* **special effects** *made the film really exciting.*

spike /spaɪk/ *noun* 1 a piece of metal with a point at one end. 2 something long and pointed.

stadium /ˈsteɪdiəm/ *noun* a large outdoor sports field with seats all round it: *a football* **stadium***.*

stage /steɪdʒ/ *noun* the part of a theatre where the actors stand and perform.

stairs /steəz/ *plural noun* a set of steps leading up and down inside a building.

star /stɑː/ *noun* 1 a small point of light that can be seen in the sky at night. 2 a famous actor, singer, sportsperson, etc: *a film* **star***.*

start /stɑːt/ *verb* to begin: *They* **start** *lessons at 9 o'clock.*

statue /ˈstætjuː/ *noun* a figure of a person or animal made of stone, metal or wood: *There is a* **statue** *of a famous soldier in the park.*

steak /steɪk/ *noun* a thick flat piece of meat or fish.

storeroom /ˈstɔːrʊm, -ruːm/ *noun* a room where goods are kept until they are needed.

storey /ˈstɔːri/ *noun* one level in a building: *This is a four-***storey** *building.*

story /ˈstɔːri/ *noun* a description of a set of events that can be real or imaginary: *Please read us a* **story***.*

strawberry /ˈstrɔːbəri/ *noun* (plural **strawberries**) a small, soft, red fruit.

suggestion /səˈdʒestʃən/ *noun* an idea of what you might do in a particular set of conditions: *Can I make a* **suggestion***?*

sweet /swiːt/ *noun* a small sugary thing to eat.

switch off /ˌswɪtʃ ɒf/ *verb* to turn off: *Please switch off the lights before you go to bed.*

switch on /ˌswɪtʃ ɒn/ *verb* to turn on: *I can't see very well. Please* **switch** *on the lights.*

sympathetic /ˌsɪmpəˈθetɪk/ *adjective* kind and understanding about someone else's unhappiness.

system /ˈsɪstəm/ *noun* a group of things or ideas working together in one arrangement: *We have a large railway* **system***.*

T

take /teɪk/ *verb* (past tense **took** /tʊk/, past participle **taken** /ˈteɪkən/) 1 to get hold of something: *The mother* **took** *her child by the hand.* 2 to carry something or go with someone to another place: **Take** *this shopping home. Will you* **take** *me to town today?* 3 to need: *I will* **take** *an hour to cook dinner.*

tasty /ˈteɪsti/ *adjective* nice to eat: *a tasty meal.*

technological /ˌteknəˈlɒdʒɪkəl/ *adjective* of knowledge dealing with scientific and industrial methods: *The computer is the result of recent* **technological** *advances.*

television /ˈteləˌvɪʒən, ˌtelɪˈvɪʒən/ *noun* (also **TV**) a machine that receives electronic signals and sends out pictures and sounds: *Turn the* **television** *on.* 2 (no plural) the system of sending and receiving pictures and sounds by electronic signals: *They were watching* **television***.*

tell /tel/ *verb* (past **told** /təʊld/) 1 to speak to someone or inform them about something: **Tell** *me what happened.* 2 to advise or instruct someone: *Dad* **told** *me to be home by ten.*

tennis /ˈtenɪs/ *noun* a game played by two or four people in which you hit a ball over a net.

tent /tent/ *noun* a shelter made of thick cloth spread over poles.

terrace /ˈterəs/ *noun* 1 a flat area outside a house where you can sit and have a drink, etc. 2 a row of houses joined together.

terrible /ˈterɪbəl/ *adjective* 1 very serious; causing you to be afraid: *a* **terrible** *accident, a* **terrible** *noise.* 2 very bad: *Your writing is* **terrible***.*

theatre /ˈθɪətə/ *noun* a building where people can go and see plays being acted.

then /ðen/ *adverb* 1 afterwards; next: *We watched a film and* **then** *went for a meal.* 2 at another time; not now: *She lived in a village* **then***, but now she lives in a town.*

think /θɪŋk/ *verb* (past **thought** /θɔːt/) 1 to use your mind to have ideas: **Think** *carefully before you decide. What are you* **thinking** *about?* 2 to have an opinion; to believe something: *What do you* **think** *of my singing? Do you* **think** *it will rain tomorrow?*

thirsty /ˈθɜːsti/ *adjective* (**thirstier, thirstiest**) wanting or needing to drink something: *Can I have something to drink? I'm really* **thirsty***.*

throw /θrəʊ/ *verb* (past tense **threw** /θruː/, past participle **thrown** /θrəʊn/) to send something through the air by moving your arm and pushing the thing out of your hand: *He* **threw** *the ball to me and I caught it.*

throw away /ˌθrəʊ əˈweɪ/ *verb* to get rid of something you don't want: *He* **threw** *the old shoes away.*

tidy /ˈtaɪdi/ *adjective* (**tidier, tidiest**) in good order, with things neatly arranged: *a* **tidy** *room.*

time travel /ˈtaɪm ˌtrævəl/ *noun* travelling into the past and the future.

time-line /ˈtaɪm laɪn/ *noun* a line which shows when events happened in the correct order.

tin-opener / ˈtɪn ˌəʊpənə/ *noun* a tool for opening tins of food.

tired /taɪəd/ *adjective* needing rest or sleep: *I felt* **tired** *after work.*

tired of / ˈtaɪəd əv, ɒv/ *adjective* to have lost interest in something because you have done it many times before: *She was* **tired of** *cooking for her family.*

tomato /təˈmɑːtəʊ/ *noun* (plural **tomatoes**) a red juicy fruit that we eat raw or cooked: **tomato** *salad.*

top /tɒp/ *adjective* highest: *Put it in the* **top** *drawer. He is the* **top** *agent.*

topic / ˈtɒpɪk/ *noun* something to talk or write about.

tour /tʊə/ *verb* to visit many different parts of a country or an area: *We're going to* **tour** *Spain.*

tournament / ˈtʊənəmənt/ *noun* a sports competition: *a tennis* **tournament**.

traditional /trəˈdɪʃənəl/ *adjective* that has been done in the same way for a long time: *a* **traditional** *family Christmas.*

translator /trænsˈleɪtə, trænz-/ *noun* a person who gives the meaning of one language in another language.

transport / ˈtrænspɔːt/ *noun* (no plural) 1 the moving of goods or people from one place to another. 2 cars, buses, trains, etc: *public* **transport**.

traveller / ˈtrævələ/ *noun* a person who is on a journey.

treasure chest / ˈtreʒə tʃest/ *noun* a wooden or metal box containing gold, silver, jewels, etc.

tree /triː/ *noun* a large plant with a trunk, branches and leaves.

trout /traʊt/ *noun* a river fish with dark spots on its brown skin, used for food.

trunk /trʌŋk/ *noun* 1 the main stem of a tree. 2 a large box to carry clothes in. 3 the long nose of an elephant.

try /traɪ/ *verb* (past **tried** /traɪd/) to attempt to do something: *He* **tried** *to climb the tree but he couldn't.*

tuna / ˈtjuːnə/ *noun* a very large fish, used for food.

U

ugly / ˈʌgli/ *adjective* unpleasant to look at: *an ugly face.*

umbrella /ʌmˈbrelə/ *noun* a piece of cloth or plastic stretched over a frame, which you can hold over yourself to keep off the rain.

uncomfortable /ʌnˈkʌmftəbəl, -ˈkʌmfət-/ *adjective* not pleasant to sit on, lie on or wear: *an* **uncomfortable** *chair, an* **uncomfortable** *bed, an* **uncomfortable** *shirt.*

untidy /ʌnˈtaɪdi/ *adjective* (**untidier, untidiest**) not tidy: *Her room was* **untidy** *- there were things all over the floor.*

unusual /ʌnˈjuːʒuəl, -ʒəl/ *adjective* not usual; strange: *an* **unusual** *hat.*

useful / ˈjuːsfəl/ *adjective* having a good purpose; helpful: *That's a* **useful** *knife.*

useless / ˈjuːslɪs/ *adjective* having no good purpose: *This is a* **useless** *knife - the handle's broken!*

V

vacuum cleaner / ˈvækjuəm ˌkliːnə, -kjʊm-/ *noun* a machine which cleans the floor by sucking up dirt.

victory / ˈvɪktəri/ *noun* (plural **victories**) an act of winning a war, a fight or a game.

vehicle / ˈviːɪkəl/ *noun* something such as a bicycle, car or bus, which carries people or goods.

video phone / ˈvɪdiəʊ fəʊn/ *noun* a telephonic instrument transmitting a picture as well as sound.

video player / ˈvɪdiəʊ ˌpleɪə/ *noun* a machine for recording and playing videotapes.

villain / ˈvɪlən/ *noun* 1 the chief bad character in a play or film. 2 a bad person; a criminal.

virtual reality /ˌvɜːtʃuəl riˈæləti/ *noun* a computer image with which you can communicate.

vitamin / ˈvɪtəmɪn/ *noun* a substance found in food that helps to keep you healthy: *Orange juice is a good source of* **vitamin** *C.*

W

wall /wɔːl/ *noun* 1 something built especially of bricks or stone which goes round a house, town, field, etc: *There was a* **wall** *around the park.* 2 one of the sides of a building or room: *We have painted all the* **walls** *white.*

wardrobe / ˈwɔːdrəʊb/ *noun* a cupboard in which clothes are hung up.

waste /weɪst/ *verb* to use something wrongly or use too much of something: *Don't* **waste** *your money.*

watch /wɒtʃ/ *noun* a small clock worn on the wrist or carried in a pocket.

wave /weɪv/ *noun* one of the raised lines of water on the surface of the sea which rise and fall.

weapon / ˈwepən/ *noun* a thing with which to fight: *A gun is a* **weapon**.

windmill / ˈwɪndmɪl/ *noun* a tall building with large sails which are turned around by the wind and used to power a machine that crushes grain or pumps water.

window / ˈwɪndəʊ/ *noun* an opening in the wall of a building to allow light and air to enter: *Please shut the* **window**.

wine /waɪn/ *noun* an alcoholic drink made from grapes.

wing /wɪŋ/ *noun* one of the two limbs of a bird or insect with which it flies.

Z

zebra crossing /ˌziːbrə krɒsɪŋ, ˌzeb-/ *noun* a set of black and white lines painted across a road to show that people who are walking can cross there when the traffic stops.

Pairwork Activities

Exercise 1 (H - page 13)

Work in pairs.

Student A: Answer your partner's questions about the puma. Ask questions to complete your table.

Example: What kind of animal is it?

Group/family	mammal - cat family
Continent	…
Habitat	all kinds of countryside
Size	…
Colour	grey or reddish-brown
Food	…
Way of hunting	alone
Other names	…

Exercise 2 (G - page 23)

Work in pairs.

Student A: Ask and answer questions to find six differences between your picture and your partner's picture.

Example: In my picture there is a small table in front of the sofa. Is there a table in your picture?

Exercise 3 (F - page 43)

Work in pairs.

Student A: Answer your partner's questions about the great footballer, Pele, and ask questions to complete your passage.

Example: 1 What did his friends call him?

Edson Arantes do Nascimento was born in Brazil in 1940. His friends called him … (1 *What?*). He was very good at football. He was only 16 when he played for the (2 *Which team?*). He scored two goals in 1958, the following year, to help Brazil win (3 *What?*). He played 1254 games for his team, Santos, and scored (4 *How many?*) goals. Then he joined the New York Cosmos. He stopped playing in 1977 but he continued to work in (5 *Where?*), where he helped to make football popular.

Exercise 4 (E - page 59)

Work in pairs.

Student A: You and your partner have similar pictures but there are six differences. Tell your partner about your picture and ask questions to find the differences.

Example: There are a few bananas in my picture, and there are six apples. Are there any apples in your picture?

Exercise 5 (G - page 73)

Work in pairs.

Student A: Answer your partner's questions about yourself. Then find out about his or her qualities. Ask what he or she has done today / this week / this month. Then give your opinions

Example: Have you finished all your homework this week? Why not?
I think you aren't very hard-working. You won't be a good teacher.

Exercise 6 (F - page 83)

Work in pairs.

Student A: Answer your partner's questions about pictures 1, 3, 5 and 7 and ask questions about picture 2, 4 and 6.

Example: He's going to play badminton. Number 2. Is the girl going to be an artist or a buisnesswoman?

Irregular Verbs

Infinitive	Past	Past Participle	Infinitive	Past	Past Participle
bite	bit	bitten	learn	learnt/learned	learnt/learned
break	broke	broken	leave	left	left
bring	brought	brought	lose	lost	lost
build	built	built	make	made	made
burn	burnt	burnt	mean	meant	meant
buy	bought	bought	meet	met	met
catch	caught	caught	pay	paid	paid
choose	chose	chosen	put	put	put
come	came	come	read	read	read
cost	cost	cost	ride	rode	ridden
cut	cut	cut	ring	rang	rung
do	did	done	run	ran	run
draw	drew	drawn	say	said	said
drink	drank	drunk	see	saw	seen
drive	drove	driven	send	sent	sent
eat	ate	eaten	shoot	shot	shot
fall	fell	fallen	show	showed	shown/showed
feed	fed	fed	sing	sang	sung
feel	felt	felt	sink	sank	sunk
find	found	found	sleep	slept	slept
get	got	got	speak	spoke	spoken
give	gave	given	spell	spelt	spelt
go	went	gone	spend	spent	spent
grow	grew	grown	stand	stood	stood
have	had	had	swim	swam	swum
hear	heard	heard	take	took	taken
hide	hid	hidden/hid	teach	taught	taught
hit	hit	hit	tell	told	told
hold	held	held	think	thought	thought
hurt	hurt	hurt	understand	understood	understood
keep	kept	kept	wake (up)	woke (up)	woken (up)
know	knew	known	wear	wore	worn
lay	laid	laid	win	won	won
			write	wrote	written

End-of-year Self-assessment

Assess yourself:

A I have no problems.

B I have some problems.

C I have a lot of problems with this.

Speaking *Writing*

☐ ☐ about animals and pets

☐ ☐ about houses

☐ ☐ about films and books

☐ ☐ about pop or film stars

☐ ☐ about spy stories

☐ ☐ about food and going out

☐ ☐ about the future

☐ ☐ about news

☐ ☐ about machines and inventions

Listening

☐ to your teacher

☐ to dialogues (on the cassette)

☐ to other students

Grammar

☐ Present simple

☐ Prepositions of place

☐ Comparatives

☐ Adverbs of frequency

☐ Present continuous

☐ Past simple regular verbs

☐ Past simple irregular verbs

☐ Quantity

☐ Obligation

☐ Future simple (*will*)

☐ Present perfect

☐ Superlatives

☐ Plans (*going to*)

Pearson Education Limited,
Edinburgh Gate
Harlow
Essex CM20 2JE
England
and Associated Companies throughout the world

www.longman.com

© Pearson Education Limited 2000

The right of Michael Harris and David Mower to be identified as authors of this work has been asserted by them in accordance with the Copyright, Designs and Patents Act 1988.

First published 2000
Eighth impression 2004

Set in 12pt Footlight Light and Eurocrat

Printed in Spain by Graficas Estella

ISBN 0582 34974 5

Illustrated by Enrique Bernabeu, Fernando Cano, Robin Edmonds, Fernando Gómez, Phil Healey, Alberto de Hoyos, Gonzolo Izquierdo and Chris Simpson.

Acknowledgements

The authors and publishers would like to thank Val Emslie for writing additional materials for World Club 1.

We are also very grateful to the following people and institutions for their contribution: Mónica Marinakis and her team from AACI; Marta Moure and Liliana Luna from Asoc. Ex-Alumnas del Prof. en Lenguas Vivas J.R.F; Nora Gervasio, Patricia Ugo, Gabriela Atrio y alumnos del Colegio Monseñor Dillon.

We are grateful to the following for permission to reproduce copyright material: Kettle Records, Post House, King Kettle, Fife for the lyrics to the song 'Air Guitar', © P. Kennedy © Some sweet music; MCA Entertainments for the lyrics to 'Sweet Home Alabama' by Lynyrd Skynyrd.

Photo Acknowledgements

We are grateful to the following for permission to reproduce copyright photographs:
Actionplus for page 62. AGE for pages 4 (c), 7 (top, middle left & bottom), 8 (top centre & top left), 10 (left), 12 (bottom left & right), 17 (left), 22 (middle left), 70, 78 (c) and 82 (right). All Action for page 37 (bottom left). All Sport for pages 43 and 108 (right). Gareth Boden for pages 59 and 109. Image Bank for pages 6, 22 (top right) and 61. Incolor for pages 4 (a & e), 8 (top right & middle right), 10 (top right & bottom right), 17 (top & bottom right) and 18 (right). Katz Pictures for page 37 (top left). Kobal for pages 27, 28 (left), 37 (middle left & middle middle), 40 (bottom centre), 67 & 77. Pictor International for page 90 (top). Popperfoto for pages 4 (f) and 47. Radial Press for pages 4 (b & g), 18 (left), 28 (right), 37 (top right & middle right), 40 (bottom right), 42, 44, 45, 78 (b) and 88. Robert Harding for pages 90 (middle left and middle middle). Stock Photos for pages 4 (d), 7 (middle right), 8 (middle left), 12 (top left), 20 and 22 (bottom). Tony Stone for pages 5, 13, 87, 90 (middle right) and 108 (left). Zardoya for pages 37 (middle left), 38, 40 (bottom left), 82 (left) and 91.

We regret that we have been unable to trace the copyright holder of the photograph on page 79 and would welcome any information enabling us to do so.